Healing What Grieves You

Four Steps to a Peaceful Heart

More praise for Healing What Grieves You

"*Healing What Grieves You* is a practical guide for people who have experienced a major loss, whether it be the death of a loved one, a divorce, a miscarriage, disability, or another life-changing event. This wonderful book is filled with a wealth of tools that can be used by shamanic practitioners, energy healers, counselors, and mental health professionals."

— Sandra Ingerman, MA
author of *Soul Retrieval* and *Walking in Light: The Everyday Empowerment of a Shamanic Life*

"Julie Lange Groth understands that grief is an inescapable experience that has the ability to break us apart but, if consciously attended to, will inevitably render us capable of putting ourselves back together again."

— Abigail Brenner, MD
author of *Replacement Children: The Unconscious Script*

"With an intuitive knowledge, gentleness, and deeply loving voice, Julie shows the reader how to work through grief with insights, journeys, and rituals that are peppered with personal experiences. She allows the reader to begin the healing process from the first sentence."

— Renata Butera
shamanic practitioner

"*Healing What Grieves You* brings the healing powers of the shaman to life. Julie Lange Groth will help you find the physical, emotional, and spiritual strength to address grief and emerge with an expanded awareness of what it means to be human."

— Fauzia Burke
founder, FSB Associates

Healing What Grieves You

Four Steps to a Peaceful Heart

Julie Lange Groth

CAPE HOUSE

CAPE HOUSE BOOKS
ALLENDALE, NEW JERSEY

HEALING WHAT GRIEVES YOU
Four Steps to a Peaceful Heart

Cape House Books™
PO Box 200
Allendale, NJ 07401-0200
www.CapeHouseBooks.com

Cover and book design by Bill Ash

Groth, Julie Lange
Healing What Grieves You: Four Steps to a Peaceful Heart

p   cm

1. Grief—Spirituality 2. Healing—Grief—Emotional States 3. Shamanism—Healing—Contemplation 4. Sacred Journeys—Self-actualization 5. Self-help—Restoration

I. Title II. Author III. Monograph

RZ 401 G187 2017   299.8144 Gr

170323

To St. Joseph, a man who knew more than most about the pain of loss and helping loved ones grieve.

Life is the flash of a firefly in the night.
It is the breath of the buffalo in the winter.
It is the little shadow that runs across the grass
And loses itself in the sunset.

— Blackfoot Crow, "Final Vision"

Contents

Contents

I. My Journey

Losing Justin

This is a book about dealing with the spiritual aspects of deep grief using the ancient tools of shamanism. From earliest times, human communities have turned to their shamans, or medicine people, for help in surviving the harsh realities of life.

The shaman had a special relationship with the spiritual realms that gave him or her the ability to access important information, guidance, and healing. Without the tools and technology of modern society, these abilities often were a matter of life and death in traditional cultures.

In tribal communities, the shaman predicted where the hunt might be most bountiful so the people did not go hungry. The shaman knew the medicine ways of plants in order to heal the sick. The people often turned to the shaman to foresee how severe the winter might be so they could decide whether to pull up stakes and migrate to a warmer clime.

Shamans the world over recognized that everything in existence— animal, vegetable, or mineral, person, place, or thing—has a spirit. The special ability of the shaman was to communicate on a spiritual level with any aspect of creation in order to access its wisdom, memory, and healing power.

Consider the memory of a stone that has witnessed creation over millennia, or the perspective of a giant sequoia tree that has been suspended in a constant dance with earth and sky, sun and air for hundreds of years. Ponder the strength of an ant that can carry many times its own weight. Think about the experiences of a river that nourishes and refreshes everything it touches.

As human beings, we can appreciate all of these natural features on a physical and mental level. But we also are spiritual beings who can comprehend the things in the natural world as fellow spiritual beings that have much to share with us. In fact, we often hear native people referring to natural phenomena in familial terms, such as Grandmother Moon, Brother Bear, and Sister River. It was the shaman's job to serve as intermediary with these "spirits" to bring help and healing to the people.

Among the commonly used tools of the shaman were ritual and ceremony, drumming, song, dance, and storytelling. Each served as a kind of prayer, a way of reaching out to the spiritual realm on behalf of the people to help them fulfill their needs, hopes, and dreams.

One of the most important roles of indigenous shamans was tending to the emotional and spiritual life of the community. Shamans helped to resolve disputes, ease troubled hearts, and restore peace during turbulent times. A combination of psychotherapist and priest, the shaman understood that the very survival of the community often hinged on the ability to live together in harmony and balance.

Shamans were especially important during times of loss and tribulation. If a sudden flood overwhelmed the village, claiming lives and property, it was the shaman who helped the people come to terms with their losses and summon the strength and resolve to go on. When a hunter was killed by a wild beast, it fell to the shaman to help the community heal from the loss of one of their own.

In the more than twenty years I have worked as a shamanic practitioner, I have experienced firsthand the power of the shamanic path to heal deep grief. In fact, my own profound loss led me into this work.

My sixteen-year-old son, Justin, died suddenly in 1993 while using nitrous oxide, otherwise known as laughing gas. He was the youngest of my three sons. His death, which was a devastating loss to our family and friends, completely flattened me. Justin was kind to everyone he met, both humans and animals, and I think he was most at home outdoors when he was surrounded by the wildness of nature.

Justin was a drummer. Back then, I did not understand the power of the drum as shamans do. In fact, I didn't know what a shaman was and held no particular spiritual beliefs. Whatever I thought I knew about anything was turned upside down in the maelstrom of emotions that follows the loss of a child.

Still, in the absence of all those comforting, accepted beliefs I learned during twelve years of Catholic school, a new awareness was finding its way onto the vacant slate of my soul. Something was happening to me that I could not explain. In my moments of greatest despair, I felt invisible hands lifting me up, carrying me from one day into the next. While I often cried myself to sleep, I sometimes woke up with a wonderful dream of Justin still fresh in my memory. When I went on my long walks, hoping to outrun my deep sadness, I sometimes encountered moments of sweet transcendence upon encountering a rainbow or a pond mysteriously covered in white feathers. I thought of these moments as grace, something I didn't really understand, hadn't earned, and certainly didn't deserve. But there they were. I felt taken care of.

Some of the greatest moments of grace came on Wednesday evenings when Justin's friends, my older two sons, and their friends got together at my house. At first we were an ad hoc support group. Many of us were musicians. Some, who already had become interested in African drumming, brought their drums, and the evening often evolved into a drum circle.

Today African drum circles happen spontaneously on beaches and city streets, but in 1993 they were something of a new idea in our little rural New Jersey town. People of all ages and backgrounds arrived with various types of percussion instruments, such as drums, rattles, and cowbells. Usually one or more experienced drummers set the rhythms, many of which have their roots in Africa or the Caribbean. Others joined as they felt moved to do so.

I had never drummed before, but this communal kind of music doesn't require particular skill or experience. Everyone has a place in a drum circle and it just feels good to play. It was easy to imagine Justin in our midst, enjoying the whole thing. I noticed something interesting:

no matter how depressed I felt before the gathering, I always felt much better afterward.

Word began to spread about the drumming circles and soon the gathering had outgrown my basement. I found some larger spaces that we could use for free and we started holding open drum circles once a month. People of all ages and interests showed up. The bigger the group, the more profound was its healing effect on all of us. As people arrived, especially teenagers, I often could read the stress of their day on their faces. When the circle was over, their faces were bright and full of energy. (Years later I read about scientific research[1, 2] proving that drumming circles elevate mental states, improve immune response, and provide other health benefits.)

Sometimes we had more than fifty people playing together, and there often were drummers I had never met before. One evening a woman about my age introduced herself to me and, in the course of conversation, told me she was a shaman. I asked what that was and she explained she was trained through the Foundation for Shamanic Studies and that she played her frame drum while "journeying" to spiritual realms.

I asked her if she would teach me and my friends to journey and she agreed. I found a gathering space in a nearby community center and invited some friends who enjoyed drumming. That afternoon changed my life. The woman played for us as we all lay on the floor, as if to meditate. A journey is somewhat like a meditation, except that the goal of meditation is to empty the mind, whereas a journey begins with a specific intention that leads the journeyer into insights, visions, experiences, or realizations that are beneficial.

I later learned that the particular rhythm the woman played put us all into a light trance, which made it easier for us to access spiritual realms and encounter loving, benevolent, helpful spirits. That day I met my first helping spirit, Turtle, who has been at my side ever since. She helps me to stay grounded and in balance. After my first journey, I was hooked. Not long after this first experience, I began my formal studies in shamanism.

At the time, I didn't realize that this work was the best possible medicine I could have chosen to heal from the loss of my son, or that it would turn out to be my soul's path in this lifetime. I was just following the bread crumbs of spirit, exploring the wonders that awaited me at every turn.

It wasn't until ten years later, while on my vision quest in the Green Mountains of Vermont, that I came to understand my soul's mission. I learned firsthand that the practice of shamanism offers powerful healing tools for healing grief and I felt a calling to bring something I call shamanic griefwork to the world.

My vision quest

I went on my first vision quest in the summer of 2003 in an isolated patch of forest in the Green Mountains near Bennington, Vermont. A vision quest, an ancient tradition, involves going alone into the wilderness to fast and pray for several days and nights while waiting for a spiritual vision or guidance.

I had not yet discovered what really called me to the mountaintop. I thought I was there to get clarity about the next chapter of my life. It had been ten years since Justin died. In that decade, I had worked hard to grieve well and much had happened. I still missed Justin every day, but I had begun a new life—a good life—and I was happy. I was doing interesting and satisfying work. I'd fulfilled my dream of becoming a writer and was involved in several deeply fulfilling volunteer initiatives. Also, I felt fortunate that my two surviving sons lived nearby and I had become a grandmother, a role that brought me a joy more profound than I ever imagined. At the age of fifty-five, I had wonderful, interesting, genuine friends. I'd even made a comfortable home with the love of my life, Lou.

I had come to look upon my life as a resurrection story created from the ashes of the deepest sorrow and gravest loss I could imagine. Yet something had been stirring in me. I knew my soul was calling me to do something more. I had come to the mountain to find out what that was. Or so I thought.

My friend Emory, an experienced and proficient facilitator of vision quests, had guided me through several months of preparation that included long phone conversations, shamanic journeys, intention setting, and physical training for the strenuous hike up Grass Mountain with three other "questers." Each of us carried a fifty-pound backpack containing a small tent and sleeping bag and the supplies we would need for four days and three nights alone on the mountain.

Halfway through this preparation process, I inexplicably developed asthma. I'd never before had asthma, but having recently done some writing about it for a pharmaceutical company, I knew it was a serious condition. When my doctor heard about my plans, she strongly advised me against going through with my vision quest. The woods would be teeming with pollen and mold spores that could trigger an asthma attack, and medical help would be far away.

"You could die up there," she said, raising my level of apprehension.

Over the weeks of preparation, I talked over the situation with Emory and did a lot of spiritual reflection as I weighed my reservations against my inner pull to go ahead with my plans.

On shamanic journeys, my helping spirits reassured me all would be well. By this time I was an experienced shamanic practitioner and teacher and had solid relationships with helping spirits. I would not presume to advise anyone else to go against their doctor's advice on a matter like this, but journeying is an approach I use to go beyond fear or ego and get to the truth of things.

So on a hot July day, I found myself trudging up the steep slopes of Grass Mountain, trusting this was something I was called to do.

Emory was leading us to the top, where we would split up, each choosing a spot on a different side of the mountain. The plan was that he would surreptitiously check on each person once a day and leave a jug of drinking water to be picked up at an agreed-upon place.

My asthma had been well controlled in recent weeks, but we had only made it about halfway up the mountain when I felt a familiar tightness in my airways. A quick tug on my rescue inhaler returned my breathing to normal, and I continued up the trail. But within a few minutes, I was again short of breath. I took two puffs on the inhaler. Emory sent the others on ahead and stayed with me while I rested.

I soon felt ready to resume my hike, but this time I wasn't able to travel more than five hundred yards before the rasping returned. I felt like a failure, unable to even complete the first part of my quest. Tears of frustration and disappointment began to flow.

"Are you ready to come down from the cross?" he gently asked. I was puzzled and a little irritated by his question. *Was he calling me a martyr? Was he accusing me of self-pity?*

With a kind and quiet voice, he explained that a successful vision quest did not require suffering. It was not a test of physical ability. I did not have to reach the top of the mountain to earn the clarity I was seeking. He suggested I return to the base camp where his wife, Tracey, would be waiting to take me to an alternate location on the mountain. The climb would be less strenuous, and she would be available to bring me water every day, as planned. I could stay there for the entire four days and three nights or return early if that felt right for me.

A tide of relief washed over me. I felt taken care of by whatever forces had called me to this experience. I bade Emory good-bye and headed back down the mountain to where I knew Tracey would be waiting. I felt lighter, almost giddy, and found myself singing all the way. All traces of asthma had vanished for the moment, and I was thrilled to be able to continue my quest.

Tracey met me below with a cheery smile and a slice of freshly baked banana bread, and after a brief rest, we headed for my new location. My breathing remained smooth and easy in spite of the rough terrain on our two-mile climb. Just as we arrived, a deafening clap of thunder threatened that rain was headed our way.

"You'd better get your tent set up," she said, nodding at the darkening sky. She turned to leave. The words had barely escaped her lips when the first fat drops fell. My little green dome tent went together quickly, but I was soaked by the time I finished. It was only three o'clock, but the heavy rain clouds and dense tree canopy made it seem like night. The rain noisily struck each leaf of every tree. Water puddled around my tent and seeped through the corners, so I huddled in the center. There would be no warm fire that night, no hot supper and no dry sheets.

My stomach growled and I thought of Tracey in her comfortable cabin in the hollow two miles away, probably enjoying a nice hot dinner. It would be a few days before food would touch my lips again. Although there were no other humans around for miles, I didn't feel alone or afraid. It just seemed like an adventure I was meant to take.

The rain continued relentlessly for the next three days and nights of my quest. Nestled in a hollow between three peaks, I was situated in a natural echo chamber in which every thunder clap was amplified. In the extreme darkness of the forest, each lightning bolt struck with exaggerated starkness. In this surreal setting, my little tent became a kind of womb, shielding me from the harshness of my environment, yet letting in enough sensory information so that I still felt like I was a part of the natural world around me.

In the darkness of the night, when the rain occasionally paused, I heard the rustle of small critters beneath the leaf litter just outside my tent. Somehow that thin membrane of synthetic tent fabric helped me feel safe, even when I heard the footfall of larger creatures moving around in the darkness.

On the second night, a storm swept through with a new vengeance. The rain came down so hard it seemed like there could be no air between the drops. This image planted the seed of an idea that quickly overtook my mind. My asthma returned. I groped in the darkness through my wet belongings, searching for my inhaler, and gulped in a big breath of Albuterol. It didn't work. I tried another, again with no effect.

Laboring for every breath, I panicked, and the panic only made it harder to breathe, which further worsened my panic. I had an emergency whistle, but no breath to use it. Even if I could blow the whistle, there was no one near enough to hear me over the deafening roar of the storm.

It suddenly dawned on me: I might die.

Then I remembered I had brought a rattle that I often used for shamanic healing work. I reached for it. My hand easily found the handle. Gasping for breath, I began to rattle and pray for spiritual help for my desperate plight. The steady rhythm of the rattling—probably intensified by fasting and oxygen deprivation—took me quickly into a light trance and I slipped into the other world, that spiritual realm of existence where awareness is heightened and the possibilities of perception are expanded. Like an express pizza delivery, the spirits answered my call.

In a flash I found myself standing at the side of a creek where my father was waiting for me. Nine years in the grave after a long, miserable bout with colon cancer, my father now appeared the very picture of vibrant good health. His smile was full of love and acceptance. Gently, he placed his hand on my back, right between my shoulder blades. His hand warmed my back and, instantly, my airways relaxed and my breathing returned to normal. All feelings of panic melted away. It was a miracle.

With my newfound breath, I passionately apologized to my dad for not being with him at the time of his death, and for not saying a proper good-bye when I saw him last, just a couple of weeks before he died. Back then, when my siblings called to say the end was near, I flew from New Jersey to his bedside in a St. Louis hospital. I was still emotionally fragile after losing Justin only ten months earlier, and I was not prepared to see my dad's horrifying physical state. He weighed barely eighty pounds.

Expecting each labored breath to be his last, I sat with him through that first night. But he made it through till morning and then another and another, and seemed to get stronger each day. For three weeks he rallied, and we had wonderful talks on an intimacy level I'd never previously known with my dad.

After a while, he suggested that the family didn't need to be at his bedside all the time. It was becoming tiring for him to always have visitors. My siblings, who lived nearby, had homes to tend and jobs to do, but I was at loose ends when I wasn't there with Dad. We all knew without a doubt that his time was near, but I just couldn't bear to wait around for the end, so I left and went back to New Jersey. I lied when I said I'd see him again in a couple of weeks as I kissed his cheek and slipped out of his hospital room. Of course, we both knew that wasn't going to happen. It was the last of many regrets regarding my dad.

I regretted we never had a very close relationship when I was growing up. I was the oldest of seven children, and I felt he saw me more as mom's assistant than as a unique little person with hopes and dreams of her own. We never seemed to have much to say to one another. Even though I was an overachiever in school, I felt he wasn't particularly interested in who I was or what I accomplished. Although he never failed to provide for my physical needs, I didn't know whether he actually loved me.

For that matter, I didn't really know much about him, either. He never talked about being yanked from school after sixth grade to help his grandparents scrape a living from their failing farm. He didn't talk about his time as a paratrooper in World War II that twice wounded him and no doubt also emotionally scarred him for life. He carefully had buried his forsaken dream of being a successful farmer, like his own father, unhealed hurts, and day-to-day disappointments as he stoically supported a family of nine without complaint.

In my vision, we were on the banks of the Musconetcong River, a place near my New Jersey home where Dad had never visited. A lifetime's worth of regret spilled from my lips. But he just smiled and gently handed me a fishing pole.

"I think you should spend less time being sorry," he said, "and more time fishing."

He took up his own fishing pole and proceeded to teach me how to fish, something he always loved to do. We spoke of happy memories and I thanked him for all the sacrifices I knew he'd made to take care of our large family. There was no longer any regret between us, only a sweet serenity and contentment. I felt truly loved by him.

I must have fallen asleep at some point during my visit with Dad, but when I woke up there were birds singing and my breathing was easy. I felt as though a great weight had been lifted from me.

My vision quest, part 2

The second day of my vision quest was long and uneventful.

During the brief intermissions between rainstorms, I ventured out of the tent to inspect my surroundings. The trees towered all around me and large boulders seemed to erupt from the ground as if the earth gave birth to them on the spot. I strung up a rope between two sturdy trees a few feet from my tent and hung my soggy clothing over it, but nothing dried before the rain returned.

The tedium of doing nothing all day was unfamiliar and uncomfortable. I missed food at first, but even more, I missed the routine of measuring out the day in the intervals between meals. On the mountain the movement of the sun was my only reference to time, and there was very little sun to be seen.

With no phone, no television, no newspaper, no conversation, no books, no chores, no calendar, no to-do list, the day became a vast, taunting emptiness. I was challenged to look below the surface of what passes for life. For the first time, I realized all the familiar supports of daily life had become a fortress protecting me from fully experiencing myself.

Late in the afternoon, the rain stopped, and I decided to build a little fire. I gathered up twigs and bark, hoping they'd burn long enough to ignite some larger pieces of wood. Everything was too wet, though. The fire kept going out. Right about that time, a couple of drops struck my head, followed by more. Soon another steady rain was falling. I gave up on the fire and ducked into my tent.

The thunderstorms came again during the second night. In the complete blackness of my tent, a storm of emotion slowly rose from my empty belly. As thunder shook the trees and all of nature seemed to be crying great sheets of rain, a long-buried guilt ripped through me like lightning, unleashing a long wail of pain and remorse. I had never uttered a sound so loud, even in the throes of childbirth.

"I let you down, Justin! I'm so sorry!" I howled into the storm again and again. "I let you down!"

In this crucible of rain and lightning, I could not hide from the horror that my son died in my own home. The storm raged on and I cried so hard it seemed like I was matching the downpour, drop for drop.

Then a vision came. Or perhaps it was a dream. Who can say? Justin was sitting beside me at a warm, crackling campfire. His face glowed in the firelight, and his blue eyes sparkled with mischievous good humor.

We talked for a long time, and it was as if death had never separated us. I saw nothing but love in his freckled, boyish face. No reproach. No regret. No blame. We embraced, and it was as if no time had passed since I dropped him off at school that fateful morning. I told him how much I loved him, and I felt his love wash over me like liquid light. Peace settled into me like a sigh. Then I slept.

The next morning I awakened with the vision still warm in my heart. Again I felt like a great burden had been lifted from me. The guilt and self-reproach I had hidden even from myself for the past ten years had at last been excavated and released. The long storm had washed me clean on the inside, readying me for daybreak and for the clarifying message of an owl.

My vision quest, part 3

On the morning of day three, the rain stopped and I crept out of my tent. Perched cross-legged on a large boulder to be off the muddy ground, I sat with a quiet mind and peaceful heart. The sun was shining and the air seemed to sparkle. As I took in the lush, moist beauty of the forest around me, a shaft of sunlight found me. At my feet, a small pool of water had collected on the surface of the boulder and, as I gazed into it, I saw the perfect blue sky reflected.

Suddenly the reflection of a large bird flew across the water's surface, and I looked up to glimpse an owl's trajectory across my campsite and into a grove of nearby trees. In a moment of sheer magic, the owl floated soundlessly down from a treetop into the leafy ground cover below. The sight of my power animal mesmerized me. I have always loved owls—their wide-open eyes that seem all-seeing and all-knowing and their otherworldly voices always pressing for an answer: Who? Who? The owl drifted in slow motion, its soft gray feathers gently yielding to the resistance of the air below. The grace of its descent held me captive until it was out of sight.

The softness of the moment was pierced by a shocked scream, quickly followed by a series of high-pitched shrieks. I supposed the pitiful sound came from some small mammal that had fallen prey to the owl.

I could not see the owl's sharp talons piercing the creature's soft flesh. I could not see who bled. But I knew the owl had struck with deadly accuracy and its prey's demise was inevitable. The small animal's squeals soon ended, but what came next clawed at my own heart. I heard the forlorn screeching of another creature—perhaps the prey's mother. Her keening seemed to go on for an eternity. The doleful cries of this bereaved animal laid open my most sacred wound. I understood its pain in a way that only a mother who's lost her own child could comprehend.

A sense of outrage bubbled up from my empty belly. *Where was justice in a world where the innocent and vulnerable are swallowed whole by circumstance? How could something as beautiful and majestic as an owl be the agent of such violence? How could a loving universe contain such a paradox? And who should be held responsible? Who? Who?*

While the emotional part of me clenched with outrage and grief, a quieter part simply observed. There was no malice in the owl. It was feeding itself using the tools with which it was born. There was nothing about its prey that deserved such a violent fate. It simply did not have the ability to anticipate such danger. Neither was the grieving animal guilty of any failure to protect its child. This death was no one's fault. Death just happens, eventually to everyone.

Suddenly I saw the metaphor in this tableau. My precious son was dead and there was no one to blame. At sixteen, he did not comprehend the danger of playing around with an innocuous-sounding substance called laughing gas, and yet it took his very breath from him. Justin's friend, who brought the tank of nitrous oxide into my own house and hid it in the basement, did not intend to harm my son. He simply didn't want his dad to find it in the trunk of his car. He wasn't guilty of any evil. Certainly no one had blamed me, the grieving mother, for failing to prevent Justin's death.

What I had not realized until arriving on this mountain is that I had indeed been blaming myself. The night before, in my tent, as thunder shook the trees and all of nature seemed to be crying great sheets of rain, the long-buried guilt suddenly had ripped through me like lightning.

Now, as the small, bereft animal's cries faded, I felt a surprising calm settle into my bones. The sun warmed my face. I could not change the past, but I could choose to see the beauty of the world more clearly. My gaze returned to the pool of water on the rock.

The sky's reflection appeared to be framed by a wreath of leafy branches, and these were circumscribed by the edges of the puddle. Only a tiny part of the broad blue sky was visible to me in this small pool. It occurred to me that my understanding of life might also be a very limited reflection of a vastness so great I could not see it fully.

Beyond the limits of my ordinary vision could be an extraordinary reality as wide and beautiful as the sky. Until that moment, I had found comfort in such boundaries. Now I was ready to behold infinity.

On a boulder in the Green Mountains

One shaft of sunlight
Transforms the whole forest.
Dewdrops become diamonds,
And the waving ferns fluoresce.
Tiny flying creatures
With invisible wings dance
In visible delight.

By now you understand that I know something about grief. Chances are, you do, too. Grief is a universal experience. It is a strong, inescapable response to a loss. Grief is pain.

Maybe it descended upon you when someone you love died, leaving an incapacitating void in your life—your spouse, your child, your parent, perhaps even a beloved pet.

The loss may not have been a death. Maybe it happened when your business went bankrupt, or when a serious automobile accident caused injuries that drastically altered your expectations for your future.

It may have been a thunderclap event that forever split your life into the times before and after it happened. Or, it may have been a torturously slow process:

- A parent slowly slipping into Alzheimer's or dementia, taking the memories that united you to a place far beyond reach;

- A valued friendship that withered, leaving you feeling lonely, devalued, and abandoned;

- A debilitating illness that robbed you of your health and independence;

- A marriage or love affair that slowly stopped working, without hope for reconciliation.

Sometimes we grieve less tangible losses that we are barely aware of:

- The loss of a childhood we never had because a parent lacked the capacity to love us well;

- The loss of self-esteem through the judgment, bullying, or criticism of others;

- The loss of innocence or sense of safety due to assault or abuse.

We play the tapes over and over in our restless minds, searching for rational explanations for why these losses happen. But rational explanations do not relieve the pain. Whatever the causes, our grief cries out for our attention and will not be ignored.

Not that we don't try to ignore it.

People struggle to muffle the pain of grief in many ways, some of them self-destructive. They may turn to mind-numbing substances, whether medication, alcohol, or illegal drugs, or obsessive behaviors, like spending endless hours surfing the internet.

Some try stalling tactics. Do any of these sound familiar?

- "I'll think about that after Christmas."

- "After my daughter's wedding, I'll take time to mourn."

- "Not now. I need to finish my big home improvement project before winter sets in."

- "The way things are blowing up at work, I can't afford the luxury of grief."

Sometimes people try distracting themselves from their feelings through immersion in constant busyness or a frenetic social life. They even may try throwing themselves into an intense new relationship in hopes that powerful new feelings will drown out the swelling tide of emotions rising within them.

But there is no escape from grief. If we do manage to bury it deeply enough to dull the emotional pain, it tends to resurface in physical or mental symptoms—heart disease, autoimmune conditions, car accidents, an inexplicable series of misfortunes, depression, anxiety, or phobias, to name a few.

We generally think of grief as an emotional state, but we also may feel it in our bodies. A heaviness in the chest that makes us sigh often and leaves us starved for oxygen. A tightness in the throat, as if we're fighting to keep a deafening sorrow from roaring out of us. A massive knot in the solar plexus, blocking all sense of personal power. A clenching in the belly that revolts against any enjoyment of food. These physical symptoms are important messages that grief is fighting for attention, crying out for healing.

My own experience bears out the physicality of grief. During the preparatory period while I worked with my vision quest guide to clarify and hone my intention for the experience, I was also working with my doctor to get my asthma symptoms under control. At the time, I didn't recognize the connection between the two. I didn't realize asthma was my body's way of telling me I had more to do on my grief process following the death of my son and my father.

In my case, it took a near death experience to break through my resistance to releasing my guilt and regret. My conversations with my dad and son dispelled the guilt I'd been carrying for a decade without even realizing it.

Through asthma, my grief had been talking to me in a very precise metaphor. My son had died of suffocation: My asthma was taking away my own breath. The guilt I had been carrying was trying to punish me by depriving me of life-sustaining oxygen.

My doctor had advised me against embarking on this solitary and physically demanding four-day fast. But I went through with it because my grief was beckoning me into a dance with my own mortality. I responded without consciously understanding why.

Within two months after returning from my vision quest, my asthma was gone, never to return. I can only conclude that because I finally had received the message that my asthma was meant to deliver, I had no further need for it.

In no way does my story suggest that a life-threatening experience is necessary in order to heal from grief. Each person's grief journey is unique and personal.

II. Your Journey

Power of intention

As a shamanic practitioner, I know that setting an intention can be a profound act of power. Formulating an intention helps me to clarify goals in my own mind and to focus and direct the energy of my spiritual practice.

I find that my helping spirits are always eager to come to my assistance when I call upon them, but by expressing my intention, I let them know just what I'm asking for. Because setting an intention is such a potent act, I choose my words carefully and precisely, knowing I am likely to get what I ask for!

So when I embark on a shamanic journey, I always trust that whatever happens during the journey will support my intention in some way. The same is true for ceremonies and rituals, particularly before embarking on a major undertaking such as going on a vision quest or teaching a new program.

I carefully set an intention for this book and performed a ritual around this process. I wrote my intention on a piece of paper and placed it in a special place in my home that honors the spiritual aspect of myself. I call it my altar and it is located in the room where I most often journey and meditate.

Then I lit a candle and repeated my intention aloud, sending it out like a prayer into the realm of spirit, a place of infinite possibility.

I drummed and sang, and soon I was on a shamanic journey, asking the spirits for help and guidance regarding this book. I didn't have to wait long. I found myself in an open field under a wide sky. In the distance I saw an iridescent speck approaching me. As it came closer, I saw that it was semitransparent and fluid in its shape. It circled around me and came to rest on my right, just outside my peripheral vision.

I asked if it was St. Joseph, who I regard as my special helping spirit for shamanic griefwork. As a child, I was taught that St. Joseph was the husband of Mary, mother of Jesus, and he always had a place of honor in the time-worn Nativity scene under my family's Christmas tree. He was portrayed as a faithful, kind, and supportive spouse and father figure. So when I began my shamanic griefwork practice and journeyed to ask for a helping spirit to assist me, I was delighted to meet St. Joseph.

The iridescent spirit who was hovering near me was not St. Joseph. Rather, I was given the understanding that it was "the voice in my ear," one that had spoken to me while I was on my most recent vision quest, my second. At that time it had said, *Don't worry. I'll take care of everything.*

I was glad to connect with this spirit again, even without a clear idea of its identity. I knew from my training and personal experience that in the spirit realms where I journey, there are only loving, benevolent spiritual beings, and so I always feel safe.

"What do I need to know as I begin writing?" I asked.

Instantly I was shown an image of a horse that had fallen and hurt its leg. I understood that this was a metaphor for someone who has experienced a big loss. Like the horse, the person who grieves has been knocked down by a profound experience that has left him or her hurt and unable to get up and move on with life.

The voice told me that, just as the horse has four legs, there are four things necessary for the horse to regain its footing. These same four things are essential for a person to recover from a deep loss.

1. The will to get up;
2. The strength to get up;

3. Balm for the wound;

4. Restoration of balance.

Each of these components will be addressed in greater detail and I'll offer some shamanic strategies and exercises for working with each one.

In a subsequent journey I again asked for spiritual input about this book and for clarity in setting a specific intention for it. This time I met a beautiful dove who told me she would be my power animal and collaborator for this stage of my work. Her energy was strong and steady but also gentle and peaceful. Two words instantly rose to the surface of my mind: comfort and healing. With those words came a strong knowing that my intention for this book would be to bring comfort and healing to those who have suffered a deep loss. May it be so.

Of course, for people who are about to begin shamanic griefwork, committing to an intention is also an important first step. Setting an intention is your spirit's expression of faith that your life has meaning and a purpose that transcends tragedy and loss. It sends a message to the powers of the universe that you are ready to put the pieces of your shattered self back together as best you can.

We need to be clear with ourselves about where we want this spiritual process to lead. Setting an intention is like entering a destination in your GPS. You can enter an address, the name of a city or neighborhood or even a particular place, such as a restaurant or golf course. But it needs to be specific.

Consider what successful completion might look like for you. What is your intended destination in this journey of grieving? How will you know your work has been fruitful? Think of some possible milestones that might indicate to you that you have been successful in your griefwork. For example, if your loss involves the death of a loved one, you might look forward to being able to:

- start a job search or return to work;

- plan a memorial service;

- wake up feeling rested most mornings;

- talk about your loved one without crying;

- go through your loved one's belongings;

- plan a trip;

- go out and enjoy yourself socially.

Everyone grieves in his or her own way, so everyone's milestones will be different. Give yourself permission to think creatively and make your intentions personal. Bear in mind that completing a program of griefwork will not necessarily mean you are finished grieving. As in my case, grief often happens in stages, with periods of rest in between. So just focus on the stage you're in right now. You can revisit your intention at any point and refine it to fit your changing emotional state and outlook on life.

It may take more than one attempt before you feel satisfied with your intention, but once you've set it, know that you have created something real, something that has your own life force in it. Energetic ripples will start spreading into the world. Say your intention out loud several times and write it down to strengthen its power.

Let's begin

B efore you read further, start working on setting an intention right now. Put this book down, settle yourself into a relaxed and comfortable position, and close your eyes.

Focus on your breath and repeat to yourself several times: "I am setting my intention for my grieving process."

As you choose your intention, consider how your life would be different if your intention were fulfilled. What change would you like to bring about? How would you feel? What would you be able to do that is not possible for you now?

If you are still early in your grieving process, your milestones may be very modest. It's fine to add new ones and cross others off your list as you go along. You can only see the view from where you are right now. As you move along the path of grieving, your perspective may change and new possibilities or desires may appear on the horizon.

Don't let anyone else set your intention for you. Other people who care about you may have their own ideas about how you should be progressing in your grief process. They may urge you to leave the house that has all those sad memories, buy some new clothes, or get out socially. Pay no attention to those "shoulds" as you set your intention. This is your process and your intention. The milestones should be entirely personal. Write down your intention and place it on your refrigerator or nightstand, or anywhere you'll see it often.

∫tart a journal

A griefwork journal is a safe space to share your deepest thoughts and feelings without fear of judgment or reproach. I urge you to keep a journal, and let the first entry you write be the intention you set for your griefwork process.

That way, whenever you open it to write about one of your insights or healing experiences, you'll be reminded to consider how you're progressing on your path of intention.

Keep your journal with you or in a place where you'll see it often throughout the day. The more you turn to it, the more wisdom you will find in it. As you progress through your shamanic griefwork, make notes in your journal about thoughts, feelings, and insights that come to you. Record your dreams in it, too.

Some people like to write poems or draw in their journals. Grief often serves up feelings too huge to be adequately expressed in ordinary language. Some other form of creative expression may better convey the gravitas of those emotions. Whatever the form, it helps to spill the feelings into some physical form, so they're not stuck inside you.

Writing poetry often was the only way I could adequately express the depth of my pain. When powerful emotions were threatening to overwhelm me, I'd sit at the kitchen table with paper and pen and let the words tumble out of me. After completing a poem, I usually felt a sense of release that left me much calmer. Here's one I wrote in the first few weeks after Justin's death[1]:

Life After Death

October, 1993

I leave a trail of heartcrumbs through the valley of my grieving
So that others may tread
Where salty tears have softened its rocky soil.
I am frozen stone,
Stunned numb by a truth
Too immense to absorb.
I am inanimate.
Each morning I wake to a new bundle of grief
Waiting to be unwrapped.
Reluctantly, tearfully, carefully, fearfully,
I rifle through its contents,
Examining its small, awesome realities,
Rummaging through hardfrozen memories,
Trying on once familiar feelings that now
Hang limp on my sapless, shrunken heart.
I sort and ponder,
Dimly conscious of the huge event
That occasions this joyless season of daily parcels,
Sorrow upon sorrow.
I am weary beyond imagining
At the effort of all this unbundling.
Sleep comes like rescue
Before the undoing has undone me.

Keeping a grief journal also helps focus your attention on the small daily occurrences that may seem like coincidences in the moment but, when strung together in your journal, can add up to form a pattern of larger meaning.

During a particularly dark patch in my journey of grief after Justin died, I was feeling overwhelmed with my troubles and broken by failure. I was dead broke and saddled with debt. My house was in foreclosure. Since I was crippled by grief, I felt little hope of finding a job. I thought I had lost my ability to find my way out of the problems and worries that were piling up in my life.

One morning I woke up determined to take my power back. I had just seen the movie, *Forrest Gump*, in which the title character dealt with his broken heart by running across the United States. Inspired, I went for a walk in a nearby county park.

Here's what I wrote in my journal that day:

This morning I rose early and drove to Schooley's Mountain Park for my walk. The sun was already hot and it felt good. As I approached the lake, a beautiful red cardinal was perched on a fence post near my path as if to greet me. I immediately thought of Justin, as I always do when I see a cardinal or a butterfly. I said a mental hello.

As I started across the wooden bridge that crosses the lake, I noticed the water was covered with something white floating on the surface. Looking closer, I realized there were thousands of tiny white feathers in the water! Molting geese probably were responsible for this amazing spectacle. But why today? Why here?

I remembered how the movie Forrest Gump had begun with the image of a free-floating feather. At the end of the movie, Forrest explained its significance. His mama had always said life was a little like a feather. We're meant to float freely and trust the wind to take us to our destiny.

I suddenly realized there really aren't any limitations on my life except for those I create in my mind. I have shelter, food, clothing on my back, and I have never had to do without any of those things. I have perfect health, sound mind and body. I have wonderful family and friends who care about me and would never let me go without. I even have my secondhand computer and the ability to use it, which I didn't have a year ago.

The word "resurrection" came to mind, and I felt a big smile overtake my face. This is what the word means! It's awakening to a new reality that was really there all along. It's a rebirth from a long gestation that only seemed like darkness, but was in fact the re-creation of the self taking place. Personal growth in the womb of devastation and loss, or what seems like it. Alchemy in the crucible of pain. Then I remembered the book, Illusions, by Richard Bach—one of my favorite books, and one that Justin had read and enjoyed very much shortly before he died. There was a white feather on the cover of the book. An omen. No doubt about it.

I had myself a great walk. As usual, I was struck with the incredible beauty of my town, Long Valley, New Jersey, and the surrounding forests and hills. I realized I was actually living one of my dreams, just by living here and having the constant inspiration of all this beauty around me. I suddenly realized that my life is really quite rich exactly as it is. Right now I can do any of the things I was planning to do later when my life got straightened out and I was healed and financially stable again. It makes no difference how much money I owe or whether I have a steady income of any kind.

Whenever you open your journal to write about an insight, a dream or healing experience that you've had, you'll be reminded to consider how you're doing on your path of intention.

ſet ſacred ſpace

As a way of showing your commitment to your grief process, you will want to create a special place in your home where you can work through the exercises and practices described in this book. It needn't be large, but it must be a relatively quiet space where you can find privacy and feel safe and comfortable.

Since this will be a spiritual process, make it a place that speaks to your spirit. Use colors that make you feel happy and peaceful. Some people like to keep the light level soft and low by pulling down the shades, turning off the fluorescents, and lighting a candle. Other people prefer natural illumination, inviting in the sun during the daytime and moonlight at night.

If you live in a place where the weather is pleasant all year long, you might want your sacred space to be somewhere outdoors. Even if you live in a small apartment and don't have your own yard, you can still bring nature into your special indoor place by laying out pinecones, feathers, stones, fallen leaves or flowers that you've collected outdoors. Your space could even be a rocking chair positioned near a window where you have a good view of the open sky or nearby treetops.

Some people like to have a picture of their lost loved one in their sacred space, but if you do this, I would suggest keeping the picture small so that it doesn't dominate the space. This space is not meant to be a shrine to the one you are grieving. It's about you.

When I am working in my sacred space, I like to burn incense or light sacred herbs such as sage, sweetgrass, cedar, lavender, copal, or mugwort. This signals to the universe that you are about to do spiritual work and that you are open to whatever messages or insights come through.

Burning sacred plants, sometimes referred to as smudging, is a practice common to many spiritual traditions around the world. It is believed to offer spiritual protection and to help clear heavy, dense energies that may be attached to a person or place. I think of it as taking a spiritual shower. By clearing away the residue of dark thoughts and emotions, I am clearing the way for light and love to flow through me. I feel better prepared to do productive spiritual work in this cleaner state.

You can buy smudging herbs at most New Age bookstores and they're also readily available online. Or if you're a gardener, you may want to grow and harvest them yourself.

Open to helping spirits

I grew up believing in guardian angels, and so the idea of having helping spirits came very easy to me as an adult when I began to learn about shamanism. The ability to call upon a power animal or teacher from the spiritual realm for help, guidance, or healing is a very real source of strength for me. I have found it helpful to have particular helping spirits for particular needs. Some appear as animals and others show up in human form or as plants, rocks, or trees. (Remember, in shamanic reality, everything has spirit.)

Each spirit brings certain gifts and abilities that support whatever I'm trying to accomplish. As you have read, for example, I have a power animal who has come to help me with the writing of this book—a dove. Since acquiring this helping spirit, it seems I always hear a dove cooing outside my window whenever I'm doing spiritual work. Hearing the dove's song and being aware of its presence brings me confirmation and encouragement that I'm on the right path.

I always suggest that anyone beginning shamanic griefwork should have a helping spirit to support them. You already may have one and not realize it. Have you noticed that you keep coming across the image of a particular animal as you go about your life? Often a power animal will keep trying to grab your attention by showing itself to you in different forms.

Before my vision quest, in which the owl spirit featured prominently, I had several atypical encounters with owls. For example, I looked out my kitchen window and saw an owl perched on my backyard arbor staring straight at me for several minutes. I had never seen an owl in my yard before.

A day later, I found the remains of a rabbit on my front porch, as if it had been left there for me as a gift. It was too large to have fallen prey to my cat, and there were no wild dogs in my neighborhood. My mind immediately went to the owl. While driving the next day, I saw a heap of feathers in the road along with the remains of an owl that had been hit by a car. While any one of these events may not have been remarkable, experiencing them on consecutive days confirmed for me that the owl spirit was trying to get my attention.

Eventually it became my helping spirit for my vision quest and I encountered it repeatedly during my time on the mountain. In mythology owls often are considered messengers of death and the afterlife. At that time I didn't know my vision quest would be so strongly involved with death and grief, but in retrospect, an owl was the ideal helping spirit for my soul work.

There are several ways to find your helping spirit. Here are a few:

- You could consult a shamanic practitioner for a "power animal retrieval." Using journeying and ceremony, the practitioner will seek out a power animal or helping spirit willing to come and help you with your grief process.

- You could set an intention that you would like your power animal or helping spirit to reveal itself to you. Then, for the next couple of weeks, pay attention for signs, as I did when the owl showed up for me. You don't have to see the animal in the flesh. You might dream of a particular animal and then see it on a cover as you pass the magazine rack at the pharmacy, or you may notice one painted on the side of a truck. Or it might even be mentioned in a song lyric that keeps running through your head. Three such experiences with a particular animal or other being could be an indication that it is your helping spirit.

- You could use some form of dousing or divination. One easy way is to buy a deck of animal spirit cards (readily available online and at New Age books stores). The deck will have a different spirit animal pictured on each card. Scatter the cards face-down on a table and pick one at random. If you have trouble accepting that this method works, keep an eye out for additional signs described in the previous techniques to confirm what the cards told you.

- You could purchase a recording of a guided meditation that will lead you to your power animal. There are many available for sale online, including a downloadable recording titled *Meeting Your Power Animal or Guardian Spirit.*[1]

III. The Four Steps

Step one:
The will to get up

For the injured fallen horse, there is no getting up until it gathers its wits and makes a focused effort to do so. So it is with great loss. Sometimes when you are reeling from the blow fate has dealt you, making a comeback is the furthest thing from your mind. There may be some mornings when you literally don't have the strength to get yourself out of bed. You can't imagine ever being OK again. You may even hear yourself say you no longer care to go on without the person (or thing) you have lost.

Especially in the immediate aftermath of a major loss, you may feel numb or frozen. You might experience yourself as existing outside the flow of life in a state of suspended animation. Everyday activities such as eating and grooming have no importance. It's as if your entire being has curled itself up into the fetal position, hoping the world will go on without you.

These are normal reactions to extreme loss and can mark the starting point of the grieving process. Unfortunately, some people don't get past this stage. We've all heard of people who follow their dead loved ones into the grave. Or people who try to literally drown out their pain by losing themselves in an alcohol- or drug-induced haze.

To survive the grief process, you have to be willing to begin it. Fortunately for most people, there eventually comes a point of readiness to begin the journey back to the land of the living. Until you reach this point, however, you are not really ready to begin the focused effort required for shamanic griefwork. However, certain shamanic healing modalities can, with the assistance of a trained practitioner, help you prepare yourself for a program of shamanic griefwork after an unhealed loss.

Soul loss

I have found that many people experience a spiritual condition shamans describe as "soul loss" after a major blow such as the death of a loved one. Soul loss happens when a traumatic experience causes part of a person's spiritual essence to leave them.

The term can be confusing because it doesn't refer to what many believe to be the person's immortal soul. Shamanic practitioners are actually talking about a person's unique life force, what some traditions refer to as *chi* or *prana*. When some life force is missing, it is more difficult for a person to live a full and creative life.

I liken the spiritual condition of soul loss to the very common physical experience called "getting the wind knocked out of you." After a physical blow or fall, the sudden pressure on the solar plexus can result in a temporary paralysis of the diaphragm that makes breathing difficult. While frightening, this condition usually requires no intervention and subsides in a few moments.

Soul loss is much more serious and healing it requires time and often the assistance of a skilled practitioner. The shaman, through ceremony and journeying on the spiritual plane, hunts for the lost soul part and returns it to its owner, thus restoring vital life force that brings about healing.

Receiving the news of a loved one's death certainly can be traumatic. I often hear people with grief-induced soul loss say things like:

- I feel like my heart has been ripped out;
- A part of me died with him;
- There's a hole within me that nothing seems to fill.

Even less severe traumas can cause soul loss, resulting in diminishment of a person's life force. Soul loss can have serious long-term physical, emotional, and spiritual consequences. Fortunately, once the missing portion of someone's vital life force has returned, the person is better able to bring his or her full self to the grieving process.

Intrusions

Blocked spiritual energy can also impede the grieving process. Many spiritual traditions consider the human body to have not only physical mass, but also a corresponding spiritual form. You probably have heard of certain mystics who are able to see people's "auras," which often look like a subtle, luminous band of color surrounding the physical form. What they are seeing is the person's "spirit body" extending a few inches or more beyond the physical body.

The well-being of the "spirit body" requires an unblocked flow of life force energy, just as an unimpeded flow of blood throughout the physical body is necessary for good health. When a clot forms in the bloodstream of a person, it can cause a life-threatening condition, such as heart attack, stroke, or pulmonary embolism.

Likewise, when there is a blockage in the flow of life force energy in the spirit body, it can cause serious spiritual, emotional, or physical problems. Shamanic practitioners sometimes refer to these energy blockages as "intrusions."

Often intrusions take up residence in a person's spirit body as the result of forceful emotion, such as anger, hatred, resentment, or jealousy being thrown at them by another person. These malicious emotions may be expressed by thought, word, or deed.

We often fail to realize the force of our words. Their power to bless or cause harm cannot be exaggerated. Even unspoken malicious thoughts can function like arrows hurled into the physical, mental, or spiritual body of a targeted person. Some indigenous shamans perceive these intrusions as darts.

When spiritual intrusions take up residence in a person, they can block the balanced flow of energy that supports well-being.

Here's an example: Harry's father dies and his sister Carrie feels she was slighted in her inheritance. A death in the family can bring up powerful emotions and open old wounds. In her bitterness, Carrie resents Harry and lashes out in anger, accusing her brother of unfairly influencing her father's last will and testament. The accusation opens a floodgate of past hurts and resentments. Her angry words unknowingly leave an energetic mark on Harry, leaving him in a weakened state with less strength to invest in his grief process.

Unaddressed intrusions can lead to a variety of serious issues. A trained shamanic practitioner, with the assistance of spirit helpers, could address Harry's condition through a technique called extraction.

World-renowned shamanic author and teacher Sandra Ingerman writes how when she first started her healing practice in the 1980s, she had great success in treating cancer, depression, and even problems such as chronic fatigue and lupus through extraction. [1]

Simply put, extraction is a shamanic act of removing energy that is out of place, in this case intrusions resulting from Carrie's angry words and feelings. I think of it as a kind of spiritual surgery, like having gallstones removed.

Unfinished business

In many traditions, it is considered important to "die a good death" so that the spirit of the deceased can be at ease in the afterlife. Even in Western society, a high value is placed on "passing peacefully." When a person dies a sudden, turbulent, or traumatic death, though, or when there are lingering hard feelings with the living, it is believed in shamanic circles that the spirit of the deceased may remain in a restless state.

This unresolved condition also may create a drag on the energy of surviving loved ones, leaving them with less strength to do their grieving. I sometimes see this issue come up with people who have experienced childhood abuse at the hand of a parent. When that parent dies, the adult child often has difficulty grieving because there are so many unresolved feelings and unhealed wounds left over from the past.

When a person carries such emotional baggage, he or she can experience extreme fatigue, depression, anger, or a variety of other symptoms.

Many shamans work with the dying and the deceased as well as willing loved ones to bring peace to the dying process and resolve unfinished business. These practitioners often are referred to as psychopomps. The term is based on the Greek words *pompos* (conductor or guide) and *psyche* (breath or soul).

Mythological and religious texts from around the world describe these spiritual guides, whose primary function is to escort souls to the afterlife. A classical example of a psychopomp in Greek mythology is Hermes, who conducted the deceased *Myrrhine* to Hades, the afterlife. Another example is the Hindu deity Shiva, who leads souls to moksha, releasing them from the cycle of rebirth impelled by the law of karma.

In shamanic practice, the psychopomp also brings special insight and deep compassion to those who are preparing for the biggest initiation of their lives—the transition into the afterlife. As the end of physical life approaches, part of that preparation often involves journeys and ceremonies to help heal old wounds and bring about forgiveness and reconciliation with the living. The practitioner also may help the dying person connect with deceased loved ones or ancestors who are waiting to welcome them to the other side.

I encourage people who are about to begin a program of shamanic griefwork to consult a shamanic practitioner and address any soul loss, intrusions, unfinished business, and other spiritual conditions that keep them from bringing their full energy to the process. See the Resources section for information on finding a trained, reputable shamanic practitioner.

Step two:
The strength to get up

If a fallen horse is too weak, it will not be able to get back on its feet. Similarly, experiencing a major loss can deplete our emotional reserves, rob us of our personal power, and even compromise our immune system.

Western medicine acknowledges that people are more prone to serious physical illness after the death of a loved one. Indeed clinical depression is so commonplace among recently bereaved people that "complicated grief" is now classified as a medical condition. [1]

While we are in this weakened grief state, we also may notice that people around us are urging us to "snap out of it"—get back to the business of life, return to our normal work schedule, and throw ourselves back into social routines. But it takes an enormous amount of physical, emotional, and spiritual strength just to meet the demands of the grieving process, let alone cope with the everyday stresses of life.

The tools of shamanic griefwork can be especially helpful in replenishing the spiritual power needed to do the hard work of grieving.

Through shamanic griefwork, we call upon helping spirits to lend us their strength and give our depleted spiritual batteries a charge. When we go on journeys, we can connect with the divine source of our own creative power and call it forth to recreate ourselves from the ashes of our past.

The following exercises may help you rebuild your own inner strength in order to better attend to your grief.

Physical grief

Close your eyes. Take some nice deep breaths, and begin to scan your body with your inner awareness. Where do you feel your grief?

It may seem like an odd notion that the emotion of grief could have a physical location. Yet I have found in leading my shamanic griefwork program that on any given day, most people can actually pinpoint it. I ask them to write down the answer to this question in their grief journals once a day. The answers can tell us a lot about what's going on in our grief process. It also gives us some insight into how blocked grief may be affecting our state of health.

Shamanic griefwork employs spiritual techniques to help us move through the grieving process with awareness and intention. So it's useful to take a moment each day to make contact with your grief and give it your direct attention. When you engage with your grief in this simple way, you can track it and gain information about how you're doing.

Sometimes the information you get comes in the form of metaphor. Metaphor is the language of the spirit. So your job is to tease out the metaphoric meaning behind the physical location where your grief is lingering.

Is it stuck in your throat? Perhaps it's telling you to speak up and express your feelings more fully today.

Is the grief in the area of your stomach? You might ask yourself what's been eating at you lately.

Is it up in your head? Perhaps there are painful memories you've been keeping at bay. See what your grief has to say to you.

Remember how I developed asthma ten years after my son died? I learned on my vision quest that the asthma was pointing out to me that there was still a layer of grief that was hidden from me and needed to be dealt with—my sense of guilt that he died in my own home and that I had failed to protect him. It was not a coincidence that my son died by suffocation, and suddenly I couldn't breathe. Quiet and muffled within me, I had still held the false belief that I let my son die and didn't deserve to draw breath.

Once I recognized the metaphor my body was showing me, I could work on healing that painful belief. Within a few months, I was free of asthma.

Often people find that their grief tends to move around. One day it's in their heart space, and the next day it might be in their big toe. That could be a sign that the grieving process is progressing well, moving from one emotional touchstone to another. But if the grief stays put, it could be telling you that you're stuck in a particular pocket of the grieving process, unable to move forward. It could be crying for attention.

Stuck grief can cause a lot of damage. Think about how many times you've heard of someone dying of "a broken heart." That's more than a poetic phrase: it can be real. There are many examples of recently bereaved people suffering heart attacks or other cardiac ailments. In fact, a medical condition called "stress cardiomyopathy," also referred to as "broken heart syndrome," is a potentially life-threatening condition that can occur following emotional stressors such as the death of a loved one. [2]

Scanning helps you be aware of your grief and what it's trying to tell you, so you can address what may be keeping you stuck and continue your healing journey.

Stuck grief

If you notice in your daily scans that the grief seems to be staying in one place in your body, this may be an indication that it's stuck there and could be blocking the natural flow of your life force. Here is a brief visualization to help you remove this blockage and disperse it in a conscious, loving way.

To make it easier to relax into this journey and all the others in this book, you may want to record yourself slowly reading the description, allowing plenty of time between each step. Then play it back as you relax and follow along.

- Sit or lie comfortably in a quiet place and focus on your breath. With each inhalation, imagine that you are taking in more and more pure white light.

- On the first couple of exhalations, breathe out any physical stress you may be carrying. Feel that stress flowing out of your body, leaving your bones and muscles soft and relaxed.

- Next, exhale heavy emotional energy you may be carrying— sadness, regret, resentment, anger, or any other one that weighs you down.

- Finally, exhale any false or limiting beliefs or critical self talk that may have crept into your thoughts. For example, *You're stupid. You do everything wrong. You're weak. You're incompetent.*

- By now, you will be feeling considerably lighter and at ease.

- Use your imagination to visualize a beautiful place in nature and spend some time enjoying this place with all your senses. It may be a place that's familiar to you, or you can create your perfect place from your imagination. Admire the bright colors. Smell the flowers. Feel the sun on your face. Hear the breeze.

- Notice a beautiful tree in the distance with a large hollow in the trunk. Go to it.

- Slip your body into the hollow and feel yourself descend below the surface of the earth.

- When you stop descending, you will be in an empty chamber where there is a flight of stairs going downward. Take those stairs.

- At the landing there is another flight of descending stairs. Head down them, too.

- At the bottom you see an opening into another place, and you know that this is the cave where the sacred fire of divine love is waiting for you. Go through the opening into the cave.

- As you enter, you immediately see an enormous, blazing fire. It is very beautiful and you are very attracted to its majesty and power. You can feel its heat on your face and you hear it crackle and pop as the flames leap and dance.

- Approach the sacred fire and introduce yourself. Ask its help in your healing process.

- Walk around the fire, admiring its beauty. As you do so, use your imagination to reach into the part of your body where grief is lodged and pull it out. It may look and feel like a dense, heavy mass of energy. Don't worry if you don't get a visual impression of this mass. Just trust that your intention to remove blocked energy will lead to that result.

- Put the grief mass into the fire and watch the flames consume it and transform it into neutral energy. Remember that you are not putting anything of value into the fire, only the built-up emotional energy that is blocking your grieving process.

- Thank the fire for helping you, and then return to your beautiful place in nature by retracing your steps.

- After you complete this journey, take some time to reflect on how you feel, and write about this in your journal.

Here is another meditation that uses the concept of being frozen as a metaphor for the effect of stuck grief in our lives. Sometimes grief can be like a coating of ice around the branches of a tree after a winter storm. It can become hard, frozen, and implacable, encapsulating our emotions like the ice grips the branches.

There is a kind of beauty and majesty in a tree coated with ice, though. Looking at itself, the tree might see that in the coldest, darkest night of winter, when it is otherwise stripped of its bright foliage, it is somehow more beautiful as it wears its icy glaze. It is breathtaking to behold.

Without the ice, the branch is stark, exposed. Shielded in its coat of ice, however, it seems less vulnerable to the biting wind.

We may look at our own cloak of frozen grief and think, *This grief is the most significant thing in my life right now. The grief gives my life the status of one who is bereaved. This grief marks me with the imprint of what I have lost. Who am I without what I have lost? Who am I without my grief?*

There is a predictability and stability in this cloak of frozen grief. At a time when we may feel we simply cannot bear the feelings that swirl like a blizzard around us, it shields us from emotion. It feels in some way like protection. We may even feel like we can go on with our lives and function reasonably well because we are protected by this armor of frozen grief.

But for a tree, there also is a dangerous brittleness in this frozenness, an inability to move without breaking. One gust of wind and the ice-coated branches might break and fall, and the tree might not even survive.

When we are like the frozen branches, when our emotions are trapped and paralyzed by cold grief, we are unable to move through life with the fluidity, grace, and vitality to fully express our unique essence. When we are frozen, we no longer have the full experience of our humanity. Frozen grief can put our very lives in jeopardy. We must allow it to melt away. The following visualization may help.

- Take some deep breaths.

- Imagine a cold winter night, right after an ice storm. You see a beautiful tree and you notice that the freezing drizzle has completely coated the tree branches in ice. They glisten with the reflected light of the full moon.

- Imagine now that you are that tree coated in ice. Experience the brittleness and stiffness of your frozen limbs. Hear your branches clatter as they bump into one another in the wind.

- Become aware that at the center of your being there is a spark of divine light always shining, even at the darkest and coldest times. See that spark of light begin to grow from your center and expand to fill up your trunk and all your branches and reach down into your roots.

- Notice that the light carries a kind of warmth that begins to melt the ice on your branches from the inside out.

- Allow all of the ice to melt away. When it is gone, notice that some tiny buds have begun to appear on your branches.

Take time to reflect on how you have been like the frozen tree in the past, and notice if you are feeling any different now. Write about this in your journal.

Here is a poem I wrote at a time when I could no longer bear being frozen in my own life. It calls for spring to come and thaw the ice on my own frozen branches. Perhaps it will resonate with you.

Spring Thaw

The frozen stream yields to the rush of melted snow.
The waterfall breaks back to life, begins to flow.
And so, the spring will come again to me, I know.
Let the warm wind blow on my life again.
I need it so.
Assembled at the doorway of a dawning day,
Remembrances of snow sting hard and melt away.
And trembling fingers frozen round my memory pray
For a warmer day.
Let a breath of spring blow this cold away.
The swollen bulbs of crocus thrust from deep below,
Their urgency at once untrussed, to rise, to grow.
And so the spring will come, it must,
To me, I know.
Let the warm wind blow
On my life again. I need it so.

Dreamwork

Throughout history many cultures have looked to certain esteemed dreamers to foretell the future or bring through messages from the divine or guidance from ancestral realms. In some tribal societies, it's customary to start the day by sitting in a circle sharing dreams and deciphering the messages they contain.

In modern times, Edgar Cayce, the renowned "Sleeping Prophet," performed readings while in the dream state for more than fourteen thousand people who requested healing. The "prescriptions" and guidance Cayce received while asleep proved remarkably effective and have been documented by Edgar Cayce's Association for Research and Enlightenment.

I have come to believe that dreams offer an avenue for our spirits to be heard. Like most people, I always have found dreams mysterious and intriguing, but after the death of my son, dreaming became a powerful tool for processing my own grief.

Within a few weeks of Justin's death, I realized I was in over my head and called a psychotherapist who had been recommended by a good friend. It was one of the wisest things I've ever done. Even though I was dead broke and had no health insurance at the time, I took a leap of faith and started seeing Barbara every other Wednesday. She was the kind of therapist who gives you homework, and so my inner work continued throughout the time between sessions. One of the tools we used was a dream journal.

Like most people, I usually didn't remember much of my dreams upon waking. Barbara encouraged me to keep a journal next to my bed and write down whatever I could remember immediately upon waking, whether it made sense or not. Even if only an image or a memory fragment remained in my mind, I found that once I started to write it down, it often would lead me to the rest of dream, like following a single strand of yarn to the entire ball.

The dreams gave my feelings a way of expressing themselves that my conscious mind would not allow. I always had had a tendency to repress all emotion. In fact, I was so out of touch with my feelings that most of the time I didn't even know I had any. I now know that this trait can be toxic to mental and physical health in the long run and that turning off emotions during the grieving process is not only counterproductive but also can be downright disastrous.

My dreams also offered me a means of communicating with Justin in ways that were healing to me. For example, here's a description of a dream I had about six weeks after Justin died:

I was shopping with someone who was Justin's father in the dream (but not his actual dad) and we were trying to select the proper transportation for him. (Justin had been looking forward to getting his driver's license within a couple of months.) His father suggested an eagle for him to ride, which seemed ridiculous to me. Then he showed me what the other kids were riding: amazing beasts and exotic contraptions beyond all imagination. Meanwhile, poor Justin had been puttering along in a very mundane 4x4. I could see that it was much too limiting for him and that riding an eagle suited him much better.

This dream left me with the feeling that a mundane, earthly existence may have been too constricting for Justin's expansive, freedom-loving spirit. It brought me some comfort to think of him in another realm, soaring on the wings of an eagle.

Another dream left me with an extremely vivid memory of playing with an eighteen-month-old Justin. Here's what I wrote in my journal.

As Justin and I wrestled and tumbled around on the floor, I carried on a casual conversation with several people who were sitting nearby. They seemed to be family members, but I only recognized one of them, my Uncle Virgil. I learned the next day that Uncle Virgil, who lived in another state, had died the previous Thursday. It came as a surprise to me because I didn't know he was ailing.

Upon waking, the sensory memory of being with baby Justin and holding him in my arms filled me with both joy and anguish. It left me with the awareness that I wasn't just grieving the sixteen-year-old Justin who had died, but also the baby and the little boy and grown man who would one day have had children of his own—and all the ages in between. But I felt there also was a deeper message.

The experience gave me the understanding that the little toddler I played with in my dream still existed on some level. I hadn't known that my Uncle Virgil was dead when I had this dream, and the fact that he was a part of this scene suggested that we were all visiting together in an afterlife realm. For me, an agnostic up to that period in my life, this was validation that what happened in my dream might be more real than I previously had thought possible.

As I did more work with dreams, I began to understand their special language. Dreams are full of metaphor and symbolism, and their deeper meanings don't necessarily match the simplistic interpretations offered in the so-called dream dictionaries that have become popular. The best way to fully understand what your dreams are telling you is to observe them over time and slowly discover the landscape, the common themes, and the inhabitants that populate your dream world.

Dreamwork became an important part of my healing journey. As I worked more and more with my dreams, I gained access to a rich reservoir of inner experience. I discovered threads of connection that ran through the entire fabric of my life. I saw patterns that repeated themselves, not only within my own lifetime, but back through my ancestry and forward into the lives of my children. I thought of life as a much larger tapestry, which helped me take a few steps back from my grief and gain a better perspective.

One of the things I was surprised to learn is that sometimes the person we dream about isn't really who he appears to be. For example, the males in my dreams often represented other males in my life. Justin and my younger brother, Ron, often were interchangeable.

This phenomenon reminds me of the movie characters in *The Wizard of Oz*. The same actors who appear in the first part of the movie in Dorothy's real life in Kansas show up again in her Oz adventure as different characters, but in similar relationships. The mean old neighbor lady becomes the Wicked Witch of the West. One of the farmhands becomes her friend, the Tin Man, and so forth.

In my life, I felt responsible at an early age for looking after my brother, Ron. I was the oldest of seven children and Ron was less than a year younger than me. By the time I was six, there were five of us. With her hands so full, my mom probably had little time to baby the older children. That's probably why Ron became very attached to me and I became like a surrogate mother to him.

He was sickly, small for his age, and bullied by the neighbor kids. I was often in the somewhat grudging role of defender, peacemaker, nurturer, and caretaker—roles I have been carrying throughout my adult life. So it wasn't so surprising that Justin often got confused with Ron in my dreams. The fact that Ron had died of heart failure a few years earlier also may have played a role in my tendency to link them.

These dreams in which Ron and Justin are switched helped me learn about one of the core beliefs that have been an issue for me throughout my life—the erroneous belief that I am responsible for everything. Because my role as caretaker was so deeply ingrained, I had transferred it to many other relationships over the years. As a result, when anything bad happened to people I loved, I instinctively felt that it was my responsibility to fix it, save them, or make everyone feel better.

Of course, this was not beneficial behavior for me or the "beneficiaries" of my caretaking. Psychologists have a name for it—enabling. My grief process gave me the opportunity to discover this false belief and confront it before it caused further damage.

Working through such discoveries was difficult and emotionally draining at times but also powerfully life changing. The more I got in touch with my feelings about Ron, for whom I had never fully grieved, the more I felt the pain of losing Justin. The process unlocked feelings of powerlessness, frustration, even rage. But the more I owned those painful feelings, the greater capacity I developed to feel good feelings again. Moving through pain lightened my heart.

Working with dreams also gave me greater insight into my relationship with my father who, like me, was an oldest child. For his own very good reasons, he, too, had had great difficulty expressing his emotions. As a result, he seemed indifferent and unapproachable to me, and I had come to believe that he just wasn't interested in me.

I craved his affection and his remoteness hurt me deeply. Over time, I distanced myself from him, both emotionally and geographically. I suspect he resented me for moving my family a half continent away, and I doubt he understood the sad dynamic between us any more than I did.

One morning, after some particularly deep work on my feelings about Ron, I awoke from a dream with these words in my head:

The birthright of my brother
was my father's uncried tears,
and my son became my brother
to validate my fears.

It took another nine years before I finally came to peace in my relationship with my dad, thanks to my vision quest. But in the meantime, working with dreams helped me to tease out the patterns in my life and better understand my feelings and relationships with Justin and others.

Daily work

Any program of self-improvement or healing requires consistency and focus. Keeping a daily food journal helps people diet successfully. An exercise journal, combined with a regular exercise routine, builds strength and fitness. Learning to meditate requires regular practice.

Likewise with griefwork, it's helpful to set aside a little time each day to reflect on how you're progressing, open yourself to whatever memories are hovering in your mind, and fully engage with any feelings that are bubbling up for attention. Even if it's only five minutes, making time for this daily reflection acknowledges the sacred trust you have made with your own spirit to honor its need to grieve. It opens up a space in your life where you can fully harvest the fruits of your grief.

Amid the frenetic rush of life, these quiet moments give you time to let go and connect with feelings that may be crying for attention. In your tranquil solitude, you can indulge in deep introspection, receive meaningful insights, and sometimes even have an aha moment!

A daily practice of planned contemplation also can free up an enormous amount of energy that you can instead invest in living. Grief can be exhausting, especially if you are walking around with your emotional radio set on "all grief, all the time." Instead, you can program your day so that a portion of time is set aside for grieving and the rest is freed up for other pursuits and plenty of much-needed rest. It's a little like making a deal with your spirit that you will give it a small portion of each day to grieve if you can have the rest of your time and energy to focus on life.

Of course, it's foolish to assume that grief always will allow itself to be corralled into a prescribed period of time. There will no doubt be times when overwhelming sadness just catches you unprepared when you're waiting in line at the supermarket checkout, watching a sentimental movie, or hearing a song that takes you back to a particular moment. Sometimes grief just happens.

But having the refuge of a daily practice can go a long way toward defusing the potential emotional land mines of bereavement. Say you catch an unexpected glimpse of someone who reminds you of your departed loved one on the street. Such an encounter could send you into an emotional tailspin from which you wouldn't recover all day, but because you have a daily practice, you can pause, take a deep breath, and allow yourself to feel your feelings in that moment. Then you can let them go, reminding yourself you can return to this experience and work through it more fully during your next period of reverie. (But be sure to return to it. Don't leave it unattended.)

When powerful emotions catch you off guard, you also can call on your helping spirit for assistance. Close your eyes and bring into your inner vision the image of your power animal, teacher, ancestor, or other loving and compassionate spirit. Imagine their gentle, healing touch. Feel their calm, reassuring energy supporting you. Open your heart and breathe in the love and light that flows from them. Ask for their help in navigating whatever is challenging you in the moment.

I have found their presence lends added insight and supports the healing process in countless ways. Many times I have called upon my helping spirits to guide me when I lost my way while driving in unfamiliar territory. My friend Lilly tells me that when she was hospitalized with breathing problems, she envisioned herself resting her hand on the furry head of her power animal, which calmed and reassured her that she was not alone in her crisis.

Foot work

After Justin died, I learned that some journeys can only be made on foot, and grieving is one of them. You can't fly across it to avoid the pain. You can't cruise through it by car and watch the landscape through a half-open window. You can't swim through the stormy tide of emotions because you'll most surely drown if you don't keep yourself grounded in practical reality.

Grieving is a step-by-step journey. Some stretches of the road are rougher than others. But every step is important. Every step has its gifts.

One of the things that helped me stay grounded in my journey was my walking routine. I lived at the top of Schooley's Mountain in the picturesque foothills of the Poconos—not a very big mountain, but challenging to walk. Picking out a three- to four-mile stretch to hike each day brought me a great deal of healing.

When I was feeling gloomy and depressed, spending time in the beauty of nature brightened my mood. The physical exertion recharged my batteries. If my mind was racing with anxiety, moving my body calmed me down and put things in perspective. Walking became a kind of moving meditation, and I sometimes experienced moments of great clarity and insight while sprinting up a steep hill or sauntering along a forest trail.

Sometimes I couldn't wait to get home to write down an idea that came to me while I was in the natural world. It happened often enough that I started carrying paper and pen in my fanny pack so I could capture the thoughts as they flowed.

Eventually, I began to look forward to the creative surges that came during my walks and I made up a little prayer to invite them. In this prayer I not only opened myself to help, healing and inspiration, but I also reached out with every part of me to invite fullness and meaning back into my life.

I am standing, here and now, in the center of the heart of God,
My feet firmly planted on the ground
And my spirit open to possibility.
My mind reaches out with curiosity,
My eyes seek out the truth.
My mouth sings out in wonder and joyfulness.
My heart reaches out with compassion and forgiveness.
My hands open up to give and to receive.
My center radiates creative power.
My belly cries out to be heard.
My womb issues out the future
As I stand here and now
In the center of the heart of God.

I found that as I said these words to myself at the beginning of each walk, they had a surprising power to shift my state of mind. Shut up alone in my house, I was prone to melancholy as my thoughts turned in upon themselves. When I went outside, I reversed that momentum. My little prayer declared my determination to reach beyond myself and open to whatever blessings were available to me in the world. The words were an expression of trust and hope, and they seemed to take on a life of their own.

Step three: Balm for the wound

J ust as the leg of a fallen horse needs to be treated before the animal can walk, a bereaved person needs to grieve to re-enter life.

In shamanic griefwork, we address the spiritual causes of various maladies that might afflict people who are grieving. In my practice, I have found that wounds of the past often bubble to the surface, asking to be recognized and healed.

The depth of emotion that we experience may excavate other deep, buried feelings and heave them to the surface like long submerged boulders. Old hurts and resentments may interrupt our sweet memories of a lost loved one, leaving us feeling guilty and confused.

Unfinished business can certainly complicate the hard work of grieving. But if we're willing to go the distance, we're rewarded with the opportunity to find peace and completeness in our relationships with people who, while physically departed, are never really gone from our lives.

Dismemberment

An initiation signifies that a person has reached a certain threshold in life and is ready to step into the next level or phase. Among the big initiations in tribal cultures are birth, coming of age, marriage, and death, and they are occasions for recognition, ceremony, and celebration within the community.

The word "initiation" comes from the same root word as "initial" and "initiate." It suggests a new beginning.

Western culture has some counterparts for certain major life initiations, such as christenings, weddings, retirement parties, anniversary celebrations, and funerals. Various religious traditions have their own coming of age practices, too, such as Christian confirmation, Jewish bar mitzvah and bat mitzvah, and the *quinceañera* on the fifteenth birthday of a girl of Latin American descent.

Experiencing a major loss also can be an initiation, although not typically one that is sought. Still, it forces us to step across a threshold into a life that is significantly different than what came before. We are changed by what happened to us.

In fact, such loss can be thought of as dismemberment. Our day-to-day reality has been torn asunder. Our old life is gone. Who we used to be is no longer. We are faced with the choice to surrender to our loss or be swallowed by a tide of overwhelming feelings.

In traditional cultures, the dismemberment initiation typically involves being taken apart or otherwise eradicated in a dream or vision. The purpose is to experience formlessness. Out of formlessness, something new can emerge. Presumably, the person being dismembered is eventually put back together with less imperfection and more power. It is a potent metaphor for death and rebirth.

After a loss has dismembered us, shamanic griefwork supports the process of putting ourselves back together in a way that incorporates all that we've learned and experienced in our crucible of pain and darkness. The work encourages us to reassemble ourselves with intention and awareness, in a way that honors the loss we have endured and the growth we have experienced.

Embracing the principle of dismemberment, and then symbolically reenacting it in a meditation, can help the healing process. You may be surprised at how much lighter and more refreshed you feel after unloading all the emotional crud that can accumulate energetically within you while grieving. Why not give it a try?

Dismemberment steps

- Put on your earphones and play a shamanic drumming recording.

- Imagine your helping spirit beside you.

- Speaking out loud, say, "I am asking for a spiritual dismemberment that will help me in my grieving process."

- Focus on your breathing. With each breath, feel yourself becoming more relaxed.

- Imagine you are on a beach, lying on the bare sand at the very edge of the water. The waves are lapping at your body. With each wave, a little bit of the sand beneath you is washed away. Then you notice that a little bit of you is also washing away into the ocean with each wave. This does not hurt. In fact, it may feel soothing, as if the ocean is caressing you and coaxing you to return to the sea and become one with it. After a time, the last traces of your body are washed into the sea. Relax into this feeling of formlessness and remain this way for a while.

- After a time, the feeling will dissipate and you will naturally return to your normal awake state. Notice how you feel. Make note of your experience in your grief journal.

It is widely understood that after being spiritually dismembered, we will instantly be put back together again, or re-membered, leaving out energetic liabilities that previously had weighed us down.

Working with stones

Journey to the sacred garden

On the path of grief, there often are some rocks in the road that serve as stumbling blocks to the healing process. If you pay close attention, you can identify what they are, understand what they're telling you, and move them out of the way.

Typical stumbling blocks might be:

- a regret that haunts you ("I should have loved her better");

- a disappointment that you can't seem to get over ("We'll never have that trip to the Galapagos");

- a resentment you can't let go of ("I felt so betrayed when he had that affair") ;

- a limiting belief ("I'll never be happy again") ;

- anger ("She had no right to treat me so badly");

- guilt ("Our last conversation was a fight").

Popular wisdom says that acceptance is the final stage of grieving, but stumbling blocks like these can stand in the way of achieving acceptance. The Sacred Garden Journey helps you identify the stones that are blocking your grief and work with them to take away their power to block your healing process.

Sacred garden journey

Repeat the steps that took you to the fire cave in Chapter V under "Stuck Grief."

- After spending some time unburdening yourself to the fire, look around and notice an opening in the side of the cave that seems to open into another place. Go to it and step through the opening.

- You have entered a magnificent healing garden. Use all your senses to take in the beauty of this place. See the vibrant colors. Smell the sweetness of the flowers. Touch the glossy, green surface of the big leaves on the trees. Listen to the songs of the birds.

- Notice that you can hear water moving nearby and walk toward the sound.

- You come upon a lily pond fed by a small waterfall. It's lovely and inviting, and you decide to step into it and immerse yourself in the healing water. The temperature is perfect and as you soak, you can feel the water drawing out any emotional or physical toxins inhabiting your body.

- You are feeling very relaxed when you decide to get out of the water. You wander over to another area of the garden where there is an open meadow.

- Standing there is a small tree, about your height. It has a bound ball of soil at its roots as if it were waiting to be planted. You understand that this little tree represents your future life, full of the possibility to thrive and grow. There is a spade next to the tree.

- You pick up the spade and dig a hole in which to plant the tree. You make good progress and the hole is nearly large enough to hold the root ball when you suddenly hear a clinking sound that tells you your spade has struck a rock.

- You know you have to get the rock out of the hole or it will block your tree's roots. You work at removing the rock, scooping soil from around its sides and using the spade as a lever to free the stone from the soil.

- At last, the rock comes free. You put down the spade and reach in to pull the stone out of the hole. As you hold it, you recognize that this stone represents a stumbling block to your grieving process. You already may have a sense of what that stumbling block is.

- Put the stone down and continue digging. You hit another stone. Remove it in the same way as the first.

- There may be several stones that need removal. Continue this process until you feel all of the stones are cleared from the hole.

- Leave the stones in a pile and return to your beautiful place in nature by retracing your steps.

After you have completed this journey, go outside and collect some actual stones to represent each of the stones in your journey. Do this in a thoughtful, intentional way without rushing. Think of a way to label or identify the various stones so you'll remember what stumbling block each one embodies over the days ahead.

Place the stones somewhere you'll be likely to notice them often. Each day, take time to sit with one of the stones, holding it in your hand and talking to it. Allow yourself to freely express all your feelings to that stone around what it represents to you. Take your time. This process could take days or weeks, or even months. It's fine to go back to a particular stone again and again if you feel there is more to be said to it.

When you feel you've come to peace with all the stones, it's time to move on to the next step, the Honoring the Stones Ceremony.

Working with stones is a powerful way to process grief. Stones have been on the earth long before humans and they store the history of the ages. People are drawn to stones and often collect them as keepsakes from their travels. Children love to collect pretty rocks and store them in boxes under their beds. It often feels grounding to hold a stone and enjoy its solidness.

Once, about halfway through an eight-week shamanic griefwork program I was leading with several people, we were working with this Sacred Garden exercise I created. A woman who was grieving the death of her husband brought one of her stones to share with the group. It was a fist-sized rock her husband had collected on some long-ago trip and left on a closet shelf. She had chosen it to represent one of the stones she retrieved during the sacred garden journey.

One day as she was holding the stone, it had split neatly in half. She showed it to us with a look of amazement. The powerful metaphor was not lost on any of us, least of all the woman who held the stone. Clearly, her work with that particular stone was complete.

Honoring the stones ceremony

Now that you have unearthed the emotional stones that have been blocking your grief process, it's time to start working with them. They are artifacts of your sacred wound and they ask for your attention. Their impact in your life must be acknowledged.

Like the stone in the New Testament that blocked the entrance to the tomb of Jesus until the time of resurrection was at hand, your stones have guarded the gates to a deep reservoir of pain and sorrow within you. They have waited for that moment of strength and safety when you were ready to rise up and face them.

The following ceremony offers a simple and heartfelt way to honor the important role the stones have played in helping you manage your grief.

Choose a quiet, private place for your ceremony, where you won't be disturbed for a couple of hours. It could be somewhere in your home, in your yard, or elsewhere in nature. Some people prefer to do this ceremony privately, but others like to have a friend or relative present as a witness.

You will need the following items:

• Your stones;

• A felt square or other cloth that your stones can easily be stacked upon;

• A votive candle in a holder;

• A handful of cornmeal and/or tobacco;

• A piece of string or ribbon.

Begin your ceremony by placing the cloth on the ground or other surface. Then:

• Play some recorded music softly in the background, or have a friend play a gentle instrument, such as a flute or violin. A Tibetan bowl also works well.

• Light the candle and place it in a corner of the cloth to invite the light of the divine to bless your ceremony.

• One by one, place the stones on the cloth to form a cairn, a Scottish word for a pile of stacked stones used as a monument or sacred shrine.

• As you place each stone, name it. Tell about what it represents, how it made you feel and what repercussions it caused in your life. Take your time with this step to fully express all the emotions you associate with this stumbling block.

• When the cairn is complete, sprinkle it with the cornmeal/tobacco offering to honor all of the feelings, memories, and experiences represented by the stones.

- Sit quietly with your cairn and acknowledge your appreciation for having cleared these stones from your path of grieving. Write in your journal if you wish. Allow yourself to feel a sense of release.

- When you feel this ceremony is complete, blow out the candle, wrap the stones in the cloth, and tie it with the string or ribbon. Keep this bundle on your altar until you are ready to do the Water Ceremony.

Water ceremony

Now it is time to release the stones that embody the stumbling blocks of your grief process. You can do this ceremony immediately after the ceremony to honor the stones, but if you are tired or don't feel ready, it's fine to put it off for another day.

In this ceremony, we use water that we have infused, through intention, with the energy of the Great Mother's oceans, the sacred womb from which all life flows. The element of water is where each of our lives began within our mothers' bodies. It's easy to see the parallels between that amniotic fluid and the waters of the oceans where life on this planet is believed to have started. It's also easy to see how water connects us with our ancestors.

All of the water that is on the planet now is the same water that existed when the first people walked the earth. The water we drink every day is also the water our ancestors consumed. The water that surrounded you in your mother's womb is the same water that cradled your ancestors. The tears that they cried and the blood that enlivened their bodies are now your tears, your blood.

From birth to death, our mother's milk, our blood, sweat, and tears, all return eventually to the Great Mother's oceans to be recycled. So it is very appropriate that we commend the stones of our grief into that sacred water, to become one with the great cycles of life.

We know that water supports all of life and we often associate it with nourishment, softness, and fluidity; the gentle way it supports us as we swim or float; and the soothing movement of waves that rock us, as in a cradle. Yet water is also powerful. It wears away mountains, cracks open enormous icebergs, and generates enough electricity to power entire communities as it thunders down a waterfall. Water also can rise up from its ocean bed with the force of a hurricane that levels everything in its path.

The stones of your grief may have seemed huge and impossible to move when you dug them up in your sacred garden, and you may have wondered if you'd ever be able to dispose of them so that you could plant the tree that is the rest of your life. But remember that in this ceremony you will be commending them to the power of the Great Mother's oceans, where anything is possible.

You also will be calling for help from your ancestors, who are connected to you by their blood, sweat, and tears that flow in the Great Mother's oceans. As you perform this ceremony, imagine your ancestors standing around you in a circle, lending you their love and guidance. Include in this circle not just ancestors you have known in your lifetime, but also those going back many generations even if you are only imagining them.

You know that your ancestors overcame many hardships. Of course, you also know that they were human and made some mistakes. Since many mental, emotional, or physical wounds may be inherited or generational, some of your ancestors may even be responsible in some way for the loss you are grieving now. But from the ancestral realm where they now dwell, our ancestors, I believe, want only happiness and fulfillment for us.

Love has replaced whatever human frailties they may have carried during their human existence that caused harm to others. Their fondest wish is for your happiness and fulfillment. If you are willing to accept their love, it can only help you to heal.

A good place to perform this ceremony is on the banks of a body of water, symbolizing the Great Mother's oceans. It can actually be an ocean or, since all water is one, it also could be a stream, pond, or lake. If you prefer to do this ceremony indoors, a large bowl of water can serve as the Great Mother's oceans.

You will need your stones, a candle, and a small amount of tobacco, cornmeal, and lavender blossoms or rose petals. I also suggest you bring a box of tissues because this is sometimes an emotional process.

- Begin by lighting the candle and asking for the waters of Great Mother that have received the tears of your ancestors to now accept the stones of your grief so that you can heal.

- Sprinkle your offerings of sage, cornmeal, lavender or rose petals on the water.

- Ask your ancestors to be present and support you in this surrendering of the stones, and then imagine ancestral beings circled around you.

- Pick up the first stone and speak out loud about what it embodies for you and how it has affected your life. You also may thank it for any lessons or blessings it may have brought, or how it served you on your life's journey. Take enough time to feel complete with this stone and ready to release it forever.

- Throw the stone into the water with as much force as you can muster. See it splash and watch the ripples move outward. (If you are using a bowl, place the stone in the water gently and wait for the water to settle around it.)

- Pick up the other stones, one by one, and do likewise with them.

- After all the stones are in the water, sit quietly for a while and observe your feelings. Allow any strong emotions that arise in you to be expressed through crying, laughing, shouting, dancing, or the like.

- After a time, a feeling of peace may settle over you, letting you know that the ceremony is complete. If you aren't feeling peaceful right away, don't worry. Sometimes it takes a little time to integrate the energy of this ceremony. It you need more time, it also could mean you have more stones to deal with in yet another round of griefwork.

- Close by blessing yourself with the water of the Great Mother's oceans and by sprinkling more offerings on the water to thank it for relieving you of the stones.

- Also sprinkle offerings on the ground to thank the ancestors who walked the earth before you for their support during this ceremony.

Having a friend or family member witness and support you in this ceremony can be helpful, but it's also fine to do this privately.

Fire journeys

In working with people who are grieving, I find that some have temporarily lost the capacity to imagine themselves ever experiencing joy or fulfillment again. It's as though their inner fire has gone out. For example, I sometimes hear people say things like, "I'll never be happy again" after the death of a loved one. Statements like that can become self-fulfilling prophecies.

A wonderfully talented musician I know became extremely depressed when his worsening symptoms of Parkinson's disease made it impossible for him to play his instrument. Music had been his life and his identity, and so his grief was profound. When he started his shamanic griefwork, his highest hope was to die before he became a burden to his family. He could no longer imagine that his life could ever again have meaning and purpose.

Fortunately, shamanic griefwork often can help to engage the imagination and awaken the ability to dream a new dream for the future and all the beauty it can hold. By the last session of the program, the man had revised his hopes and dreams, and his intention was to live each day to the fullest. He discovered that although he could no longer play the banjo, his primary instrument, he could still play guitar. He got his band back together and they resumed public performances.

Stoking your fire

In the natural world, there are four cardinal elements: earth, water, air, and fire. Everything on earth is made up of these elements, including our bodies. Our spirits and emotions also carry aspects of the elements.

For me, the earth element represents our ability to be grounded, stable, and practical, while our watery nature is more flowing, dreamy, and attuned to the spiritual. The air element relates to our ability to imagine and aspire, to reach for the golden apple, while fire sparks our passion and ignites our creativity.

Each of us needs all four elements to live a balanced, happy, and healthy life. But grief can throw us off-balance, and often the element that is most off-kilter is fire. When we are grieving, it can sometimes seem like our inner fire has gone out, leaving us in a dark, cold place.

Just as fire often is used to heat up the air that causes a hot air balloon to inflate and rise, we need our own inner fire to fill us up with the life force so we can get up and move through our days. It's our inner fire that brings sparkle to our eyes and color to our cheeks. Fire ignites our passion and creativity. It enables us to feel compassion for ourselves and others. So awakening our inner fire is an important part of healing after a loss.

In ancient times, fire was thought to be a precious gift from the gods that allowed the people to survive. Fire enabled them to keep warm in the winter, scare off predators in the night, and see in the dark. Since they had no matches, it wasn't so easy to get a fire going, especially in wet weather. Rather than wait for lightning to strike or for the rain to end, a new camp sometimes would borrow some fire from a neighboring village.

It was considered a sacred trust for a "fire carrier" to bring back glowing coals as an act of service to the community. [1] Among the Lakota Sioux, the ember was placed in a hollow bison bull horn, where it could continue to smolder for more than a week while being transported. Once it arrived in the neighboring village, that small coal would generate a mighty blaze, probably accompanied by great celebration, and the fire would keep the tribe warm and safe for a long time.

As a griefworker, I sometimes think of myself as a fire carrier for those who have suffered a deep loss, helping to reawaken their inner fire that may have gone dark. In griefwork gatherings, we use ceremony and creative expression to help stir the glowing embers of our spirits and help them remember what if feels like to shine bright. Here are some practices you can do on your own or with a small group to wake up your fire and remember the brilliant, radiant being that you are.

Journey to retrieve fire

This is an ideal journey for times when you feel sluggish, tired, heavy, moody, or generally unhappy with yourself. These feelings may indicate your inner fire is low and the flames need to be stirred back to life.

The intention for this journey is to go to the sacred fire of divine love that is always blazing in your other-world cave and retrieve some for yourself. (This is the same cave where you unburdened yourself to the fire.)

- Sit or lie comfortably in a quiet place and focus on your breath. With each inhalation, imagine that you are taking in more and more pure white light.

- On the first couple of exhalations, breathe out any physical stress you may be carrying. Feel that stress flowing out of your body, leaving your bones and muscles soft and relaxed.

- Next, exhale any heavy emotional energy you may be carrying— sadness, regret, resentment, anger, or any other one that weighs you down.

- Finally, exhale any false or limiting beliefs or critical self talk that may have crept into your thoughts. For example, *You're stupid. You do everything wrong. You're weak. You're incompetent.*

- By now, you will be feeling considerably lighter and completely at ease.

- Use your imagination to visit your beautiful place in nature and spend some time enjoying this place with all your senses. Admire the bright colors. Smell the flowers. Feel the sun on your face. Hear the breeze.

- Notice the beautiful tree in the distance with the large hollow in the trunk. Go to it.

- Slip your body into the hollow and feel yourself descend below the surface of the earth.

- When you stop descending, you will be in an empty chamber where there is a flight of stairs going downward. Take those stairs.

- At the landing there is another flight of descending stairs. Head down them, too.

- At the bottom you see an opening into another place, and you know that this is the cave where the sacred fire of divine love is waiting for you. Go through the opening into the cave.

- As you enter, you immediately see an enormous, blazing fire. It is beautiful and you are attracted to its majesty and power. You feel its heat on your face and you hear it crackle and pop as the flames leap and dance.

- Approach the sacred fire and introduce yourself. Ask if you may take some of the fire to help you in your life.

- Follow your own inner guidance regarding how to take the fire into yourself. You might use your hands to reach in and pull one of the flames into your heart space. Or you could just breathe it in and feel its vibrant energy filling you.

- If you feel the impulse to step into the fire, don't be afraid. Consider it an invitation to merge with this powerful element in a way that's very healing. Remember, this is all occurring in your mind and spirit.

- When you feel sufficiently "filled up" with fire, thank the spirit of fire for this precious gift.

- Return to your beautiful place in nature by retracing your steps.

- After you complete this journey, take some time to reflect on how you feel and the qualities that fire brought back to you. Write about this in your journal.

Creative journeys

Many people find that creative activities help them manage their grief without stifling the deep and powerful feelings that sometimes threaten to overwhelm them. The great composer Ludwig van Beethoven wrote some of his most powerful works while he was deeply depressed over his advancing hearing loss.

The renowned American author Joan Didion wrote *The Year of Magical Thinking* during the period immediately following the death of her husband, John Gregory Dunne, in 2003. It has been acclaimed as a masterful work on the theme of mourning.

Francisco de Goya painted some of his most memorable works after surviving two near-fatal illnesses, one of which left him mostly deaf. In the years before his death, he produced what are now known as the "Black Paintings," which ultimately helped to elevate Goya to higher ground within the painting world.

After the death of his beloved wife, famous sculptor William Wetmore Story created his beloved *Angel of Grief* sculpture to serve as her gravestone. This deeply evocative work has been widely imitated by other artists.

For me, writing was powerful medicine as I mourned the death of my son. It seemed that only poetry held the power to express the powerful storm roiling within me. Ordinary language lacked the gravitas to convey the depth of my sorrow.

At that time, I did not consider myself a writer. I only wrote when I needed to vent or express strong emotions that just couldn't be talked out with a friend. It didn't matter to me then whether my writing was any good, because I imagined no one but me was ever going to see it.

When the losses started piling up in my life, I had just acquired a secondhand computer. In a way, it became my therapist and confidant. In those days I owned my own advertising agency, which had begun to flounder after eight years of success. I had just learned that my dad was suffering from advanced colon cancer and the prognosis was not good.

Then my close friend Angela, a talented graphic designer, suddenly lost her only brother, John, to a heart attack. He was a bright, young doctor in his mid-thirties, and the two had shared an apartment in New York City while he was in medical school. John's death knocked the wind out of Angela. When she talked about losing her brother, she said it was as though her heart had imploded. She compared the grieving process to assembling a patchwork quilt—recovering little bits of herself, one by one, and sewing them back together. We decided to create a children's story on that theme. The plan was that I would write the book and Angela would design and illustrate it when she was stronger.

I completed the story while I was driving back to New Jersey from a trip home to Illinois to spend time with my folks. My dad was recovering from surgery for his advanced colon cancer and my mom was having long-delayed back surgery. I helped with driving and everyday chores, hoping to ease the burden on my siblings who lived nearby.

The day before I was scheduled to return home, I got a call from Angela: her mother had just died of a heart attack. It was as if she had decided to follow her son into the grave. My sorrow for my friend was overpowering, and I felt helpless to offer any support or comfort. *What words of sympathy could bring solace to someone who has just lost two members of her immediate family in such a short period of time? What could I possibly do to help heal her broken heart?*

As I drove the twelve hundred miles across the Midwestern prairie, the jumble of emotions flowing through me gave way to a steady stream of ideas for our book. *This was what I could do for Angela*, I suddenly realized. Perhaps completing our book would help her express the depth of her sorrow and weave together some kind of meaning from the strands of incomprehensible tragedy.

The words flowed as if I were channeling them from an invisible source. Every few miles I had to pull the car over to the shoulder of the road and jot down plot elements, phrases, or sentences. By the time I pulled into my driveway in New Jersey, the story line was complete and much of the content was written. Little did I know that by the time I had finished the story, it also would be about me. Within a few weeks, Justin was dead and my own heart was imploding.

The story was a fable about a little earthbound angel in search of his lost heart. We called it *Luca's Lost Heart* and, although the story was never formally published, I now know that it already had been written in the stars long before Angela and I ever thought of it. Here is how it begins:

Luca's Lost Heart

There is something very magical that angels and children have in common, and that thing is a heart. A heart is actually more of a place than a thing, and in that place the most wondrous transformations occur.

It is a place as vast as galaxies, spinning with limitless possibilities and dreams that rocket out of one another like fireworks on a starry night. And yet, it is a place that closely cradles the tiniest of secrets in its private crannies, where nothing is ever misplaced.

All things ever created first begin in the heart. And no matter how large or small its owner's size, the capacity of a heart is most miraculous, for it holds inside it all the feelings and memories of an entire lifetime in a space no larger than a sticky bun.

So naturally, when the terrible thing happened to Luca and his heart was so suddenly lost, he no longer felt like himself. It was as if all the light had gone out inside him.

Luca had just enough light left to know that he missed his heart and wanted it back very much. And so one day he put on his backpack, tied his sneaker laces in double knots and set off to find it.

∫tep four:
Restoration of balance

A horse needs all four of its legs to support a stable and steady gait. But for the person who grieves, restoring balance may be an elusive goal. At the beginning of the grief process, we may feel consumed with the loss we have experienced. This state is the epitome of imbalance. Everything in our lives is eclipsed by the vacancy that loss has carved out of us. Work, play, relationships, eating, sleeping, even hygiene seem trivial. Hopes, dreams, ambitions, and aspirations we once held dear are dwarfed by the enormity of our grief.

For me, one of the great gifts of shamanic journeying is new perspective. In an expanded mental state, exaggerated emotions gently give way to an ability to see a situation with a calmer spirit and fresh eyes.

Here's an example that demonstrates how a fresh perspective can restore balance. While the loss I am about to describe may seem trivial compared with the major loss you have experienced, it helps demonstrate my point.

When I was well into my fifties, I was laid off from a job I absolutely loved. I had only been working there for two years, but I had regarded the job as a genuine gift from the spirits, an answer to the heartfelt prayers of my vision quest. I felt valued and appreciated at work, but the nonprofit that employed me lost a major part of its funding. All nonessential staff had to go. The news came as a shock.

My instinctive reaction was to go home, get into bed, and curl up in a fetal position. Emotionally, I felt I had been punched in the gut. Fear washed over me. *Who would hire a woman my age? How long could I survive on my meager savings and unemployment income? How would I ever find another job that was so perfect for me?*

I stayed in bed for two days. Fortunately, this state of immobility gradually gave way to my natural resilience. Through shamanic journeying, I was able to regain some perspective on my job loss as a single event within the wide horizon of my life. My helping spirits showed me how to experience myself as a spirit on a physical journey—a capable, creative, resourceful person who always had landed on her feet, regardless of any adversity. Working with my helping spirits, I came to realize that the loss of my job obviously was a sign that it was time for the next step on my path. I needed to widen my view to see new possibilities to explore.

With my sense of balance restored, I was able to be patient and strategic with my job search. I was no longer sending out the energy of anxiety and desperation with each resume. Instead, I felt myself opening and welcoming new possibilities.

After three months of job hunting and interviewing, I was offered three great positions in one week. The one I chose was in the environmental field, an area to which I felt strongly attracted but for which I was not very well qualified. Or so I thought.

The nonprofit company that hired me happened to need someone with my particular skill set, just when I was available and looking for employment. It turned out to be my dream job, allowing me to contribute my experience and abilities to a worthwhile cause while continuing to learn and grow.

In the course of my job search, my former employer (feeling regret for cutting me loose so abruptly) offered me free life counseling sessions. I hit it off so well with Shannon, my coach, that we decided to develop a series of workshops together combining life coaching tools and shamanic journeying. Our program was called *Heart Callings: Creating Your Career from the Inside Out*, and it gave me a great deal of joy to share this program with others several times before Shannon's husband accepted a new position in another state and she moved there with her family.

Loss of innocence

Here's another example of how classic shamanic tools and techniques can help to regain balance, in this case in the aftermath of childhood sexual abuse.

Mary, a woman I know very well, had lost a precious piece of her childhood self when she was molested by a close friend's uncle when she was ten years old. She did not feel safe confiding in anyone about the rape. Instead, feeling alone, betrayed, and overwhelmed by her secret, she blocked the experience from her memory for decades.

Imagine the mental and emotional energy it took to hold such a traumatic memory at bay. Even though Mary was not consciously aware of what had happened to her, the loss was very real and had caused deep damage with which she had never dealt. Without knowing why, she became emotionally numb and unable to trust or form close, meaningful relationships.

In shamanic terms, Mary had experienced soul loss. The trauma had caused a part of her unique spiritual essence to flee. Psychologists would call it disassociation. For more than forty years, she had been attempting to live with part of her own personal life force walled off and unavailable to her.

Through a series of shamanic journeys, she came to remember the rape without having to re-experience the strong emotions that accompanied it. In her journeys, she was cared for by helping spirits in a way that she never had felt emotionally supported as a child. The wisdom of her spirit allies helped her, over time, to understand how the trauma had contributed to her lopsided way of relating to people and had led her to certain life choices that didn't support her happiness.

Assisted by a trained shamanic practitioner using a healing technique called soul retrieval, she ultimately was able to reclaim the lost part of herself that had fled at the time of her rape. Gaining this broader, clearer perspective of her past, present and future helped Mary heal and restore the emotional balance that had been missing for most of her life.

Since major losses often involve an element of trauma, soul loss often is present in people who grieve. Soul retrieval is an important tool for healing grief and always should be considered when beginning shamanic griefwork. Regaining the spiritual essence that was lost at the time of trauma will enable the person who is grieving to bring more energy and creativity to the process.

Repacking your suitcase

Being able to reimagine yourself as whole and healed is important in regaining your balance after a deep loss. In the wake of such a loss, you are becoming someone you have never been before. But you still carry certain traits and gifts with which you were born and many of the qualities and abilities you have acquired throughout your life.

This next journey invites you to inventory your life and celebrate the parts of yourself that you value. It also allows you to consciously choose the pieces of yourself that you no longer wish to carry into the next chapter of your life.

In this journey, you imagine you are in your bedroom. An open suitcase is lying on the bed and you are sorting through the contents of your closet. Each item of clothing hanging on the rack symbolizes something significant about you and all you've experienced.

Your closet is full of moments, experiences, gifts, talents, and aspects of yourself that have been a part of your life. Maybe there's a ball gown representing your love of dancing. You might find hiking boots that represent your kinship with the great outdoors. A maternity dress could represent your nurturing self. A business suit might indicate your skill for organization and management. There also might be garments that remind you of dark periods, challenges with which you struggled, and relationships that were lacking.

As you go through your closet, notice how you feel about each item. If you're moved to try on one or more items, do so. Consider whether it's something that still reflects who you are or aspire to be. Have you outgrown it? Does it support you in your journey forward?

Does it make you feel good about yourself? Is it something you would want your child to find buried in your closet?

Whatever you wish to keep in your life, pack it in your suitcase for the journey into your future. If it adds love, self-worth, vibrance, joy, and learning to your life, bring it with you. But if it no longer serves you or who you are becoming, leave it in the closet. As you complete this journey, see yourself closing the suitcase, picking it up, and heading out the door into your perfect future.

After this journey, sit quietly for a while and notice how you feel. Think about the items you chose to keep and what they mean to you. See if you can describe yourself based on the contents of your suitcase. Write about all this in your journal. Know that you always can add more items to your suitcase, and you always can remove things you decide you no longer want in your life.

Vision mapping

Now that you have a suitcase bulging with aspects of yourself that you want to carry with you into your future, it's time to express all that beauty in a more tangible way by creating a vision map. A vision map looks like an ordinary collage to the casual observer, but it has a much deeper significance. This personal work of art will encompass not only qualities, gifts, abilities, and traits from your past and present self, but also new experiences, relationships, opportunities, and gifts that you want to invite into your future life.

Even if you feel you are not artistic, you'll have no problem with this exercise. You can't do it wrong. Start with a sheet of 11x17-inch paper, or larger, of any color, and a stack of magazines, catalogs, calendars, and newspapers or any printed material from your recycling pile that has lots of pictures. Turn on music you enjoy and let your juices flow.

Start searching for images that appeal to you on a gut level. When you see something you like, snip or tear it out. Don't think about anything too much at this point. Just pick what attracts you. After you have a nice pile of images, go through them again and think about what gifts or aspirations the images might represent in your life. What did you like about them? Do you connect with them emotionally? Why?

Remember the journey on which you filled your suitcase with your personal qualities, gifts, abilities, and traits from your past and present? Do any of the images you have clipped remind you of those things? What new things would you like to bring into your life? A new love relationship? A more meaningful career? Deep friendships? Financial abundance? Look for visual ways to express those desires.

There is no need to depict anything literally. The images you pick can be visual metaphors. For example, if you are a person who likes to be of service, an image of a honeybee could be a fitting symbol. Maybe you like to build things or work with your hands, so you could choose a picture of a hammer or wrench. If you desire a life of peace and serenity, you might show a beautiful landscape or the universal peace symbol. If you want to embody physical vitality, you could use bright splashes of warm, vibrant colors.

You also can incorporate favorite photos of yourself, people, pets, or occasions in your life that you want to carry forward into your perfect life. Start to assemble your collage when you have ten or more images to put on your vision map. Arrange them on the sheet of paper in a way you find pleasing and then begin to attach them with a glue stick, rubber cement, or the like. It's OK for things to overlap. Neatness and orderliness do not matter in this process. Give yourself permission to be bold and flamboyant.

As you go along, you'll probably think of additional qualities or desires you'd like to include, so feel free to go back to your printed materials to search for more images to add. You can also use a marker to add words, phrases, favorite quotes, and poems.

If you're a scrapbooker, this process probably will come very easily to you and you may even have bits of ribbon, buttons, or other trimmings on hand to add to your vision map. But resist the urge to add anything just for the sake of aesthetics. Everything on your collage should have meaning.

You don't have to complete this process in one sitting. It's fine to add things to it over weeks or months as you come across images that speak to you or new aspects of yourself emerge that you'd like to have reflected on your vision map. Consider it a living work of art that can grow along with you.

Take time to bask in the radiance and energy of your vision map and allow yourself to love the beautiful life it is calling in for you. By making this collage you have created a work of visionary art. It is an act of power. The collage is communicating to the creative powers of the Universe what you intend to manifest in your life. So remember the old saying, "Be careful what you wish for!" Make sure that what you weave into your vision map is something you will welcome into your life.

Many traditional cultures believe that artists are shamans. What they paint or weave or sculpt is not a representation of something that already exists, but rather a process of creating what will become real. For example, when a Huichol artist in Mexico makes a yarn painting depicting an ear of corn, it may very likely be a visual prayer to *Jicuri*, the peyote plant, which is considered the plant of life and harmonious relations with the gods, so that there will be sufficient food to feed the community.[1] When the Shipibo women in the high Andes of Peru weave ancient designs into cloth, they sing corresponding songs to the plant spirits to bring harmony and healing to the people.[2]

Hang your vision map in a place where you'll see it every day, perhaps on your refrigerator or next to your bed. Let it be a daily reminder of who you are and who you are becoming. It will nurture your healing process and you will be amazed at how your vision begins to unfold over time.

I made my own vision map during the first few years after Justin's passing. It was a time when I had experienced a true life "dismemberment." My youngest son had died and left me with an empty nest. My business had gone bankrupt. My home was in foreclosure and my car had been repossessed. I had lost my identity. Almost all traces of my former life were gone.

The items on my vision map included, among others, a warm, welcoming home where I could surround myself with family and genuine friends, a loving relationship, meaningful work, vibrant health, service to others, music, and lots of plants and flowers. I hung my vision map on the wall near my bed, where I would see it every evening before going to sleep and every morning upon waking.

Within five years, everything on my vision map—and so much more—had become part of my life.

Value of community

Death rituals are a part of all human cultures. In Western society we are accustomed to funerals that typically involve the embalming of the deceased; a period of visitation in a funeral parlor, often accompanied by viewing of the remains; and some kind of memorial ceremony or religious service. Funeral customs provide an opportunity for family and friends to grieve together and support those most affected by the death.

Often I have heard people say they hate funerals. Some refuse to even attend one because it makes them feel too sad or "creeped out." These rituals, however, are an important part of successful grieving.

Unfortunately, many Western funerals are sterile and overly subdued. Visitation periods in funeral parlors are generally limited to a couple of hours and it's customary to speak in hushed tones. The bereaved often are sedated, depriving them of the opportunity to fully experience the powerful emotions that people normally feel when a loved one dies. As a result, the full expression of those feelings often is delayed to a time when the bereaved are alone and there is no loving community to lend support.

Death rituals in traditional cultures are much richer and embrace the full range of human emotions around grief. The entire community comes together and the proceedings often last for days, however long it takes to ensure a complete experience for both the living and the dead. It is understood that everyone in the community has a role to play in ensuring that the departed has "a good death."

In *Ritual: Power, Healing and Community,*[3] Malidoma Patrice Somé describes the typical burial rites of the Dagara people in West Africa where he was born. When a member of the community dies, the village is divided into three groups, each of which has a role to play in the rituals following a death. One group comprises musicians and singers who improvise a performance depicting the history of the deceased. This reenactment honors the dead as they depart to the realm of the ancestors.

The second group comprises mourners—those who are most deeply affected by the death—and containers. The job of the containers is to protect the mourners and keep them confined within the ritual space where they are allowed to fully express their grief.

The third group comprises all the other villagers. They pay their respects to the deceased, who is dressed in full ceremonial regalia and seated in a kind of shrine. The people "throw" their grief into the sacred space of the shrine. Two women elders, who attend to the corpse, collect all the grief and load it onto the soul of the dead as it readies for its departure to the realm of the ancestors. Somé writes:

> Without grief, the separation between the living and the dead never actually shifts into that stage in which the living accept the fact that a loved one has become a spirit. The departed loved one consequently never arrives where death commands him or her to go and, therefore, becomes angry with the living. If there is no expression of grief, it will affect the dead and the living detrimentally. ...

> It is the presence of the community that validates the expression of grief. This means that a singular expression of grief is an incomplete expression of grief. A communal expression of grief has the power to send the deceased to the realm of the ancestors and to heal the hurt produced in the psyches of the living by the death of a loved one. ...

> Grief is in fact owed to the dead as the only ingredient that can help complete the death process. Grief delivers to the dead that which they need to travel to the realm of the dead—a release of emotional energy that also provides a sense of completion or 'endedness,' closure. The sense of closure is also needed by the griever who has to let go of the person who has died. We have to grieve. It is a duty like any other duty in life.

In *The Smell of Rain on Dust*,[4] Martin Prechtel echoes the importance of community in supporting those who grieve. The author of several spiritual books, Prechtel grew up on a Pueblo Indian reservation in New Mexico and eventually settled in Santiago Atitlán, a Guatemalan village where he was initiated as a Mayan shaman.

He tells the story of how after a burial, the newly bereaved wander through the streets of the village in a slow procession, weeping, wailing, and raging with sorrow. Friends and relatives surround the grieving parties as they make their way through town, providing a safe container of song and prayer.

"A tribe is necessary even if it's just to be a kind of resilient nonjudgmental human basket, against which the griever is able to thrash," writes Prechtel.

The emotional outpouring might continue all day, and at the end of it, the bereaved are each carried home by as many as seven people because the weight of their grief makes them so heavy.

"It was unthinkable to stop the griever from yelling," he continues. "No one ever tried to 'heal' him, or hush up any inappropriate blather he might spout. The people knew grief was not a sickness nor any kind of affliction, but a pain-filled testament of courageous praise they bore whomsoever their heart had lost."

That local culture understands that the living owe the dead such full-throated grief. Such unfettered expression of love and praise for the deceased helps the living heal and the dead move toward the afterlife.

As Somé and Prechtel so eloquently explain, community can play a valuable role in the process of grieving so as to fulfill the contract between the living and the dead. Unfortunately, in our Western culture many people do not have a spiritual community to support them in their grief rituals. But it is still possible to create a powerful ceremony to fill that void by bringing together a small circle of friends and family.

The following is one example of how people can come together to allow those who are grieving to express their powerful feelings within a safe, loving, and supportive community.

Healing and remembrance ceremony

This ceremony can be done in a natural setting or indoors. My favorite place is next to a body of water, but any quiet location will work well. It's especially appropriate for someone who is grieving the death of a loved one, but it certainly can be adapted for any major loss.

While this ceremony is especially effective in a group setting, such as a grief support group or memorial service, I also have found it healing to do it alone, with only the trees to bear witness.

You are ready for this ceremony after you have fully excavated and worked with all the "stones" that have blocked your grief process. If you still have a lot of unfinished business with the person who died and/or who caused you to suffer a loss, you may want to put this ceremony off until you've done more work with the stones.

Elisabeth Kubler-Ross, in her landmark book, *On Death and Dying*, describes five emotional reactions associated with the experience of grief. They include denial, anger, bargaining, depression, and acceptance. If you are working within the context of these five stages of grief, this ceremony is appropriate as you are moving into the acceptance stage.

If you are grieving the loss of a person, the purpose of this ceremony is to celebrate and honor the ways that person enriched your life. What special qualities did you admire or appreciate? What were the gifts of that person's presence in your life? What lessons did you learn from your relationship, even if they were hard lessons?

In the first part of the ceremony, you will speak out loud about the person you are grieving and officially say good-bye. Understand that you are not saying good-bye to your love for them or your memories of them. It doesn't mean you will stop missing them. The ceremony simply acknowledges that you have worked hard to grieve well, and, to the best of your ability, arrived at a place of peace and understanding.

This is not a time for whitewashing the facts. In many funeral services, the dead seem to suddenly attain sainthood as the assembled recite a litany of their better qualities. But none of us is a saint, and relationships with parents and other close family members often are complicated and less than optimal.

It's important in this ceremony to tell the truth. I once had a therapist who admonished me not to "put whipped cream on horse sh*t." As I learned then, doing so accomplishes nothing and certainly isn't doing any favors for the deceased. Telling the truth cannot hurt the dead, but varnishing the truth can shortchange you of the full value of this ceremony.

It's OK to acknowledge that your love for the deceased was big enough to encompass even their character flaws and human frailties, and the ways you may have suffered because of them. But also honor the ways your life was blessed by them and perhaps forever changed by them. Give specific examples. Tell stories.

Here's what you'll need for this first part of the ceremony:

- Some sage or incense in a form suitable for burning;
- A cloth to serve as an altar;
- A candle;
- Photographs or keepsakes that remind you of the deceased;
- Ten to fifteen flowers that remind you of the deceased, even if just by way of their color;
- Poems or readings that fit the occasion and the way you feel about the deceased.

Also lay out the items to be included in the second part of the ceremony:

- A plate containing one or more favorite foods of the deceased;
- A beverage the deceased enjoyed.

Steps for the first part of the ceremony

- Lay out the photographs and/or memorabilia on a cloth.
- Light some sage or incense.
- Place the candle on the cloth and light it.
- Play some soft music and focus on your breathing as you gather your thoughts. (It's OK to use written notes if you wish.)
- Begin by reading a poem, quote, or passage. You can read it or have someone else officiate.
- Pick up one of the flowers and talk about the deceased, focusing on a particular trait or aspect you remember. Place the flower on the cloth near the photographs or, if the ceremony is next to a body of water, throw the flower onto the water and watch it float for a moment.
- Pick up another flower and say more about your relationship about the deceased and what it meant to you. Again, place the flower on the altar cloth or throw it in the water.

- Repeat this process until you have no more to say.

- Close this part of the ceremony with a reading or poem.

The second part of the ceremony is what I like to call a Spirit Feast. It involves eating and drinking the deceased's favorite food and beverage in your loved one's memory. You might think of it as a farewell toast. It also might remind you of the practice of "taking communion" in many religious communities.

As you do this part of the ceremony, imagine the ancestors of the deceased are circled around, welcoming him or her into the afterlife. By partaking of the food and drink laid out for the ceremony, you are breaking bread with the family, a vast family that extends far back through time and space.

This ceremony can be especially meaningful if it's performed in a group setting. You could invite other people who have experienced major loss, and each person can place photos and/or symbolic objects on the altar. One by one, participants can step forward, place their flowers on the altar or in the water, and talk about the deceased or the loss they have suffered. It can be very empowering to have others silently witness this process.

There should be plenty of flowers and enough food and drink for everyone to share. After the first few bites and sips, close the formal part of this ceremony with a reading or song. Then allow the mood to become lighter as everyone continues to enjoy the food and drink. At this time people might start to share memories and tell funny stories.

If you are doing this ceremony alone, finish as much of the food and drink as you wish and then blow out the candle to complete the ceremony. In an outdoor setting, you might consider leaving a small portion of the food for the animals to enjoy on behalf of the deceased.

Readings for the healing and remembrance ceremony

I've collected quite a few poems and songs that I like to use for this ceremony. Here are a few of my favorites.

Final Vision

By Blackfoot Crow

Life is the flash of a firefly in the night.
It is the breath of the buffalo in the winter.
It is the little shadow which runs across the grass
And loses itself in the sunset.

St. Teresa's Prayer

Attributed to St. Thérèse of Lisieux and St. Teresa of Avila

May today there be peace within.
May you trust God that you are exactly where you are meant to
be.
May you not forget the infinite possibilities that are born of
faith.
May you use those gifts that you have received, and pass on the
love
that has been given to you.
May you be content knowing you are a child of God.
Let this presence settle into your bones, and allow your soul the
freedom
to sing, dance, praise and love.
It is there for each and every one of us.

A famous poem entitled "The Guest House" by Rumi, the Sufi mystic, is a beautiful addition to this ceremony.

I often turn to the book, *The Prophet*, by the Lebanese-American poet Kahlil Gibran, which contains a treasure trove of poems celebrating life and death, love and family. I am particularly partial to his poem "Speak to Us of Love."

There also are several poems in John O'Donohue's book, *Anam Cara*, that work well for this ceremony. One of my favorites is "Beannacht," the Gaelic word for "Blessing."

All of these works can be easily found on the internet.

Suggested songs

These songs are well known so it's easy to find recordings of them in music stores or online:

- "Amazing Grace"

- *"Dona Nobis Pacem* (Grant Us Peace)"

- "Happy Trails to You"

The tree of the rest of your life

Remember that hole you dug in your sacred garden, the one from which you cleared all those stones? It's ready now. The earth has been cleared and prepared. The hole is big enough and deep enough to hold that tree that's been waiting to grow into your best life.

This next meditation takes you back to the garden to plant it. As usual, find a nice quiet space where you will not be interrupted or distracted. Make yourself comfortable.

- Close your eyes and take a few deep breaths. Set the intention that each breath will take you more deeply into your meditation.

- With each inhalation, imagine yourself filling up with light. With each exhalation, imagine yourself releasing all stress and heavy emotion.

- Return to your beautiful place in nature, and go to the tree with the hollow trunk. Step inside and allow yourself to descend.

- When your descent stops, notice the flight of stairs going downward and follow them. When you reach the landing, notice a second flight of stairs and go down those, too.

- At the bottom, see the portal leading into the fire cave and step through it.

- The fire welcomes you warmly. It's like an old friend greeting you. Feel your love for the fire and experience it with all your senses. Interact or dance with it if you feel guided to do so.

- In the wall of the cave, see the opening that leads to your healing garden. Once again use all your senses to take in the beauty of this place. See the vibrant colors. Smell the sweetness of the flowers. Touch the glossy, green surface of the big leaves on the trees. Listen to the songs of the birds.

- Hear the sound of the waterfall flowing into the lily pond and move toward it.

- You are happy to come upon the sparkling water of the lily pond and you smile, remembering how it held you so gently in its healing embrace when you were here last. You've come a long way since then.

- If you wish, go ahead and get into the water and enjoy its beauty and healing power. You can feel the water drawing out any emotional or physical toxins inhabiting your body.

- When you are ready, get out of the water and head over to the area of the garden where you dug the hole to plant the tree that is the rest of your life.

- Still standing there is a small tree, about your height, with its root ball wrapped in burlap, waiting to be planted. It is so vibrant and strong, ready to embrace every opportunity to thrive and grow. Notice its shape, foliage, and color.

- Next to the hole are a pile of dirt, a spade, a bucket of water, and a wheelbarrow full of compost.

- Take the spade and use it to move some of the compost from the wheelbarrow into the hole to make a soft bed for the tree's roots.

- Pour some of the water into the hole to soften the soil.

- Take hold of the tree by its trunk and gently lower it into the hole.

- Shovel more compost onto the root ball and add more water.

- Shovel the dirt from the dirt pile to finish filling the hole and tamp it down with the back of your spade. Pour the rest of the water onto the area around the trunk.

- Now stand back and admire your handiwork. You have done your best to give your tree a solid footing. You've made it easier for it to sink its roots deep into its new life. You have given it your blood, sweat and tears.

- Your tree looks healthy and radiant, strong, and eager for life. You feel yourself falling in love with it.

- Draw closer to your tree now until you are right up against it, holding the trunk in both hands.

- Your feet are in the mud at the foot of the tree, and you seem to feel roots coming out of the bottom of your own soles, sinking into the rich, nourishing earth.

- You feel the bright sunlight on your skin and scalp and you feel your entire being reaching upward, toward the sky.

- You feel yourself swaying as a breeze moves gently through your hair. The leaves of the tree also dance.

- In this perfect moment you feel the pulse of life moving through you, the urge to become and grow and flow. You feel at one with your tree and with the mud and sun and wind. You feel at one with all of creation and its limitless possibilities.

- Remain with your feelings for as long as they last and then open your eyes.

- Record your experience in your journal.

If you have a yard, consider buying a young sapling tree of the type you planted in your sacred garden and find a place to plant it in your yard. In the weeks and months ahead, spend time with your tree and let it remind you of the beauty of the life you are creating for yourself.

If you don't have a yard or can't plant a tree yourself, you could:

- Have a tree planted in a park or garden as a memorial to your loss, and go visit it from time to time; or

- Draw or find a painting or photo of a tree like the one in your sacred garden and give it a prominent place in your home.

IV. A New Self

Rebirth

In the depths of our grief, something new is being born in us. Grief is the dark mother delivering from her womb of sorrow an unfolding version of ourselves. This new version experiences dimensions of emotion that the old version could not. The new version has collapsed and stretched and suffered and learned in ways that leave us changed forever.

We emerge from our grief—if we have grieved well—with expanded awareness of what it means to be human. If we have shown ourselves compassion for our own suffering, we will have developed more compassion for others. If we have seized the opportunity to sift through the myriad emotions and memories that flood our hearts and spirits while grieving, we can mine the golden nuggets of truth that may enrich the rest of our lives.

As Judith Viorst writes in her book, *Necessary Losses*, "The people we are and the lives that we lead are determined, for better or worse, by our loss experiences."

Life is likely to bring many losses, great and small, and grief always has more to teach us about ourselves. Sometimes a new loss thrusts us deeply into incapacitating sorrow over a previous loss that was never adequately grieved.

I discovered this when Lex, my dog, died after a very long and happy life of seventeen years. He was sick so his passing came as no surprise. Yet the depth of my reaction caught me off guard. I was literally doubled over with sadness, and the tears swelled and flowed like emotional floodwaters for days.

I came to realize that my outsized sorrow over Lex's passing had a lot to do with my still incomplete grief over losing Justin eight years earlier. Lex started out as Justin's dog, and I can still picture that moment in the pet store when the clerk placed that furry, squirming bundle of puppy energy into his arms. When their gazes met for the first time, the story already was written.

Lex was my loyal companion in the days and years after Justin passed. He accompanied me on walks and rode shotgun when we ran errands in the car. There was a perpetual grease stain on the chair upholstery next to the spot on the floor where he always plopped down next to me. In every way, Lex was the very definition of unconditional love. No wonder his passing triggered a big new wave of grief about losing Justin.

After Lex passed, I found that my empathy was much greater for others who were bereft over the death of a beloved pet. Often, we find that the losses we have shouldered in our lives deepen our capacity for compassion and our ability to support others in their grief. We develop a deep knowing of what words to say and when to remain silent. We learn the momentous gift of just bearing witness to another's suffering.

Grief also teaches us about the difference between being strong and being stoic. It takes a lot of energy to be stoic, to hold back emotion and soldier on through life as the losses pile up in a dark, locked closet of our being. While stoicism may look like strength from the outside, it often comes from a place of fear and shame. Stoics may resist exposing their vulnerability and fully experiencing their pain, and so they bury it where it can't be seen and judged by others.

Sometimes true strength is in surrender, allowing deep feelings to flow freely and act themselves out in unruly ways. There is strength in allowing grief to disrupt schedules, in failing to fulfill others' expectations, and inexplicably bursting into tears in the supermarket checkout lane.

Willingly giving ourselves over to our grief is a radical act of courage. It is faith in life itself, a deep trust that, just as the natural cycles of life decree that spring always follows winter and light follows dark, joy will follow sorrow if we cooperate.

Another loss, another opening

In *The Year of Magical Thinking*, Joan Didion tells us of a friend's letter of consolation that she received after her mother's death. The words of the former Maryknoll priest described perfectly what she was feeling. The death of a parent, he wrote, "...despite our preparation, indeed, despite our age, dislodges things deep in us, sets off reactions that surprise us and that may cut free memories and feelings that we had thought gone to ground long ago. We might, in that indeterminate period they call mourning, be in a submarine, silent on the ocean's bed, aware of the depth charges, now near and now far, buffeting us with recollections."

Our most primal relationship is with our mother. For the first nine months of our existence, we experience the world through the lens of her body. We begin life, quite literally, as a part of her that only a trauma as violent as childbirth can set free. So it's not surprising that the death of our mother can unleash deep, confusing and unexpected feelings.

About halfway through the completion of this book, my own mother died suddenly. I was not prepared for how her death flattened me. She was nearly ninety and had juggled a number of severe health problems for years, so I'd been mentally preparing myself to lose her at any time. But I soon learned my heart was not prepared at all.

Mom and I had a complicated relationship, and it had grown more strained in recent years. Deep inside, I felt she had never approved of me, and in her eyes, I may have given her ample reason to feel that way. Of her seven children, I was the oldest, the one who was supposed to set a good example for the younger ones. The one who was supposed to be mom's surrogate. But after nineteen years of toeing the line and never breaking a rule, that mold started to crack.

I skipped the church wedding and eloped one weekend without her knowledge, breaking a cardinal rule of eldest daughters and my Catholic upbringing. I then moved to Memphis and later San Francisco, putting a lot of distance between my family and me to follow my new husband's Navy assignments. Instead of staying home to raise my kids, I pursued an education, and then a career, entrusting their care to a succession of babysitters.

I left my solid and financially rewarding corporate career and started my own advertising agency, a leap of faith that must have appeared foolhardy to someone of my parents' conservative generation. After twenty years of marriage, I got a divorce, something almost unheard of in our large, extended family.

To top it all off, I later embraced the practice of shamanism, something my mom conflated with devil worship.

When we were together, I struggled to focus on our shared interests and common ground. But I have to admit she had a hard time with many of my life choices. Living twelve hundred miles apart made it easy for us to tiptoe around our issues most of the time. For decades I chose avoidance as the path of least resistance but, as I ultimately learned, unfinished business tends to survive death, especially when it involves such a primal relationship as the one between mother and daughter.

When my brother phoned to inform me of my mom's passing, I flew home. My siblings and I attended to funeral arrangements, the burial, and then the solemn sorting out of her belongings and dividing them up among family members. It was a great comfort being together as we busied ourselves with these myriad tasks. We told stories, shared memories, and shed tears.

While no childhood is perfect, we all realized that we were very blessed growing up in our family. Our parents provided well for us. As siblings, we shared a lot of love and laughter. But as I returned to my home in New Jersey after the funeral, I could tell there were still some burrs lodged under the saddle of my grieving heart.

Giving myself time to grieve, I canceled the workshop I was scheduled to lead on my first weekend back home, but I decided to go ahead with my second vision quest, which I had planned months earlier. This time, instead of going deep into the forest, I stayed at a retreat center in the nearby Pocono Mountains, which I knew would be deserted by midweek. It was a place I knew very well. I often taught classes in shamanism there. I deeply loved the land and the spirits who dwell there.

My original reason for planning this time alone had been to get a clearer vision of who I was to become in my cronehood, the ancient term for the elder stage of a woman's life. Once again, though, my plans gave way to the unexpected. My spirit clearly had more pressing work to do.

Over several days leading up to the vision quest my heart was restless and my dreams were troubled. An awareness of my own mortality stirred me in a way I'd never experienced. Suddenly, I was an orphan. There was no one to remember me as a baby. Powerful emotions were building in me, like steam in a teakettle getting ready to blow. The day I left for the retreat center, my stomach felt like a churning concrete mixer and my heart grew heavier with each beat.

By the time I arrived, I was so weighed down with grief I could barely walk. I left my things in the car and, with labored breath, made my way to the pond where I often had meditated. I greeted the spirits of the land and water, asking for their help and support on my quest, and then dropped in a relieved heap onto a bench where I closed my eyes in prayer.

Slowly, a sense of peace filled me, letting me know that I had come to the right place to heal. Within an hour, my entire being felt lighter, and then I opened my eyes to a most amazing sight that could have come from an animated Disney film. I was surrounded by my helping spirits, showing themselves in physical form!

An eagle soared lazily overhead. A dragonfly darted above the surface of the pond. A turtle poked his head out of the water to say hello, and a honeybee was hovering over the crown vetch in front of me. A deer grazed not twenty feet away, and a crow cawed from its perch overhead. The tree next to me was filled with cardinals, reminding me that my ancestor spirits often showed themselves as a tree of cardinals. An ant, another of my spirit helpers, was crawling across my foot, and as I looked down at it, I saw clover, a favorite plant spirit helper, peeking out from beneath my sandal.

To complete the scene, there was a four-leaf clover next to my foot, waiting for me to notice it. Encircled by these loving beings, I felt completely held and supported in my quest of healing.

Over the next four days and three nights of fasting, journeying, journaling, and ceremony, I went through all the steps of shamanic griefwork described in this book. I cried many tears as I worked faithfully with the stones, squarely facing my anger, disappointment, resentment, and hurt feelings, and honoring all the ways they affected my life.

Finally, I capped off my time there with a ceremony of healing and remembrance. One by one, I threw flowers into the pond to honor my happy memories and favorite gifts from my mother. I thanked her for giving me life and for the lessons I learned from our relationship, even the hard ones.

I remembered her love for the little animals that showed up in her yard and her mighty talent for growing flowers and vegetables.

I remembered how she used to dress me in pretty little frocks that she sewed on her Singer machine when I was small.

I remembered her fierce independence and how much it meant to her to have her own home and her own money.

I remembered how pretty she was and how proud I felt when people told me I looked like her.

I remembered how she loved music of all kinds, how she often broke into song as she went about her housework, and how I would often chime in.

Most of all, I realized for the first time that I was conceived out of love and a full-on celebration of life itself. My father had just returned from the gore and devastation of World War II, and my mom had been holding a place in her heart for him as she waited to start their life together. For them, my birth must have been an affirmation that life could be beautiful and good again. What a privilege for me, as a tiny baby, before the quick succession of six more children, to have felt completely precious and adored.

I returned home from my quest with the clear awareness that, despite the warts and wrinkles in our relationship, my mother was an extraordinary woman in many ways. She probably was exactly the mother I needed to teach me the things I came into this life to learn. In grappling with my unresolved issues with her, I had rediscovered my deep appreciation for my life, every little bit of it.

My heart was much lighter and my spirit felt peaceful. Shamanic griefwork had been a powerfully healing experience for me. But I don't mean to imply that I was finished with my grief process that day. Often there are multiple layers of grief that can only be dealt with sequentially, like peeling back the layers of an onion.

I have done more grieving for my mother since then, and after you complete your griefwork process, you also may discover over time that there are more pieces of grief that have been hiding in the corners of your awareness. Those pieces may be linked to buried memories, erroneous beliefs, or unfinished business that you did not even know existed before you started your griefwork process. If that happens, you may find it helpful to repeat some of the griefwork steps. Be patient with yourself and take whatever time is necessary. This is not a race. It is sacred work.

I wrote this poem one night while sitting in my backyard under a velvety, star-spangled sky. For no particular reason, a sudden upwelling of pure joy filled my entire being. I felt a deep knowing that my life, for all its moments of frustration, confusion, disappointment, and pain, was a gift beyond all imagining:

I have a belly full of stars
I am the stars
I am the spaces between the stars
I am the light streaming from my fingers
I am the dust trailing from my footfalls.
I am the juice of life
The blood
The guts
The nectar
The rain
The ocean.
I am the sparkle in my eye
And the reflection there of you.
I am the smile that forms around my breath
I am the breath that caresses you.
I am the agony and the ecstasy
The fire that burns the flesh
The rain that douses the fire
The sand that swallows the rain
The wind that scatters the sand
I am the song of each cell
Each thought
Each ripple of love moving through space and time
As if there were none.
I am all the songs together
I am song.
I am the wail of the mother giving birth
The whale crying out for the ocean.
I am the crack in the sidewalk that yields to the flower.
I am the kiss of tomorrow meeting today,
the unending embrace that joins infinity.
I am the sigh following the storm,
The storm chasing its tail
The tale of the shaman chasing a spirit that never moves.
I am the bird soaring in a sky that does not know
any difference between itself and the bird.
I am this body
With its head aflame

And its heart in the deep of the ocean
And its belly full of stars.

Perhaps if I had not experienced great grief in life, I never would have come to that moment of bliss. Had I not been willing to dive into my own dark nature, I might have missed this opportunity to be awestruck by the luminous delight of being alive.

I know in every cell of my body that this unconditional joy is available to everyone, regardless of past misfortune and heartache. My wish is that on your grief journey you will surrender ever more deeply into a place of grateful fullness where the radiance of your beautiful life will unfurl.

Resources

Shamanic practitioners

- Sandra Ingerman's Shamanic Practitioners list,
  http://www.shamanicteachers.com/practitioners.html
- The Foundation for Shamanic Studies Shamanic Healing and
  Services list, https://www.shamanism.org/resources/services.php

Shamanic drumming recordings

- *Shamanic Journeying: A Beginner's Guide*, Sandra Ingerman, http://tinyurl.com/gmowb2x
- *Shamanic Journey Solo and Double Drumming*, Michael Harner, http://tinyurl.com/hs5xlme

Suggested readings

- Ash, Lorraine. *Life Touches Life: A Mother's Story of Stillbirth and Healing*. Troutdale, OR: NewSage Press, 2004.

- Cowan, Tom. *Fire in the Head: Shamanism and the Celtic Spirit*. New York, NY: HarperCollins, 1991.

- Harner, Michael. *The Way of the Shaman*. New York, NY: HarperCollins, 1980.

- Ingerman, Sandra and Hank Wesselman. *Awakening to the Spirit World: The Shamanic Path of Direct Revelation*. Louisville, CO: Sounds True, 2010.

- Ingerman, Sandra. *Medicine for the Earth: How to Transform Personal and Environmental Toxins*. New York, NY: Three Rivers Press, 2000.

- Ingerman, Sandra. *Soul Retrieval: Mending the Fragmented Self*. New York, NY: HarperOne, 1991.

- Prechtel, Martin. *The Smell of Rain on Dust: Grief and Praise*. Berkeley, CA: North Atlantic Books, 2015.

- Somé, Malidoma Patrice. *Ritual: Power, Healing and Community.* New York, NY: The Penguin Group, 1993.

Notes

I. My Journey

Losing Justin

1. Barry B. Bittman, Lee S. Berk, David L. Felten, James Westengard, et al., "Composite effects of group drumming music therapy on modulation of neuroendocrine-immune parameters in normal subjects," *Alternative Therapies in Health and Medicine*, 7.1 (2001): 38-47.

2. Sandra Dickey Harner, "Immune and affect response to shamanic drumming," *ETD Collection for Fordham University*, Jan. 1, 1995, http://fordham.bepress.com/dissertations/AAI9520609 (accessed Apr. 2016).

II. Your Journey

Start a journal

1. Julie Lange, *Life Between Falls: A Travelogue Through Grief and the Unexpected* (New Jersey: BookSurge, 2008).

Open to helping spirits

1. Sandra Ingerman, *Meeting Your Power Animal or Guardian Spirit* (Colorado: Sounds True, 2014), http://www.soundstrue.com/store/meeting-your-power-animal-or-guardian-spirit-5916.html (accessed Apr. 2016).

III. The Four Steps

Step one: The will to get up

1. Sandra Ingerman, "The Power of Shamanism to Heal Emotional and Physical Illness," http://www.sandraingerman.com/sandrasarticles/abstractonshamanism.html (accessed Apr. 2016).

Step two: *The strength to get up*

1. Sidney Zisook, Katherine Shear, "Grief and Bereavement: What psychiatrists need to know," *World Psychiatry*, vol. 8 (2009): 67-74, http://onlinelibrary.wiley.com/doi/10.1002/j.2051-5545.2009.tb00217.x/full (accessed Sept. 2016).

2. "Stress Cardiomyopathy Symptoms and Diagnosis," Johns Hopkins Medicine, http://www.hopkinsmedicine.org/heart_vascular_institute/condition s_treatments/conditions/stress_cardiomyopathy/symptoms_diagnosi s.html (accessed Apr. 2016).

Step three: *Balm for the wound*

1. Katharine Berry Judson, *Montana — The Land of the Shining Mountains* (Chicago: A.C. McClurg, 1912).

Step four: *Restoration of balance*

1. "Huichol Art," *The Huichol Center for Cultural Survival*, http://thehuicholcenter.org/huichol-art (accessed Apr. 2016).

2. Howard G. Charing, "Communion With The Infinite — The Visual Music of the Shipibo tribe of the Amazon," *Ayahuasa*, Sept. 5, 2008, www.ayahuasca.com/spirit/primordial-and-traditional-culture/communion-with-the-infinite-the-visual-music-of-the-shipibo-tribe-of-the-amazon (accessed Apr. 2016).

3. Malidoma Patrice Somé, *Ritual: Power, Healing and Community* (New York: Penguin Books, 1997).

4. Martin Prechtel, *The Smell of Rain on Dust: Grief and Praise* (Berkeley, CA: North Atlantic Books, 2015).

Glossary

Cronehood – The elder phase of a woman's life when she is venerated for experience, judgment, and wisdom.

Dismemberment – A spiritual initiation in which a person is figuratively taken apart to achieve a state of formlessness and purity.

Extraction – The removal by a shamanic practitioner of displaced energy, sometimes called intrusions, from a person's body.

Initiation – A spiritual rite of passage or advancement to a new level of skill, understanding, or awareness.

Journey – The most universal practice of indigenous shamans, involving out-of-body travel to non-physical realms to meet with benevolent spirits to gain guidance, information, help, and healing.

Shamans – Medicine men or women who serve their tribes or communities by acting as intermediaries or messengers between the human and spirit worlds.

Smudge – Burning sage or other dried plants in a ceremonial manner for the purpose of purifying a space or releasing dense, heavy energy from a person, place or thing.

Soul retrieval – The restoration of part of a person's vital spiritual essence that was lost due to trauma.

Acknowledgments

As this book continues its journey into the world, I express my heartfelt thanks to those individuals who have made it possible, including:

- My parents, Ruth and Bud, who gave me life and a wonderful family, and who taught me so much about love, responsibility, joy, and grief;

- My wonderful husband, Lou, whose love and understanding supported me throughout my times of grief and the writing of this book;

- My precious children and grandchildren—Joe, Jon, Justin, Janine, Laurel, Kaeli and Margot—who have been my greatest teachers;

- My teachers, Sandra Ingerman and Michael Harner, who introduced me to the path of spirit and the ways of the shaman;

- My editor, Lorraine, for her brilliance, gentleness, and competence;

- My friends Colleen, Dee, Dini, Fauzia, Lisa, and Renata for their encouragement and thoughtful insights.

I give thanks to Great Spirit, to Mother Earth, and to all the plants, animals, and minerals who feed my spirit, mind, and body. I give thanks to all the loving beings who help, guide, teach, and heal me. I am grateful for this once-only day, for my life, my family, my health, my home, and my work.

May peace prevail on earth through the power of love.

About the Author

Julie Lange Groth thinks of her life as a collaboration with the creative forces of the Universe.

An experienced shamanic practitioner and teacher, she is the founder of Ravens Drum, which offers workshops, advanced studies, gatherings and spiritual healing services.

Julie is a graduate of the Foundation for Shamanic Studies three-year program as well as Sandra Ingerman's two-year teacher training.

Additionally, she has studied with shamans from a variety of traditions. She is a Reiki II practitioner and a 4th degree Paqa in the Andean tradition. She also is certified in advanced Pranic Healing.

Teresa Pyskaty, Whirling Dervish Design, LLC

As a grandmother, Julie finds that children are natural shamans as well as uninhibited artists and she hopes to help others connect with the forgotten child and shaman within themselves.

She is a member of the Foundation for Shamanic Studies and the Society for Shamanic Practitioners.

Healing What Grieves You is Julie's second book. Her first, *Life Between Falls: A Travelogue Through Grief and the Unexpected*, chronicles her healing journey after the accidental death of her 16-year-old son in 1993.

Visit Julie at www.julielangegroth.com .

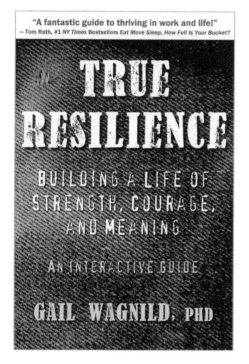

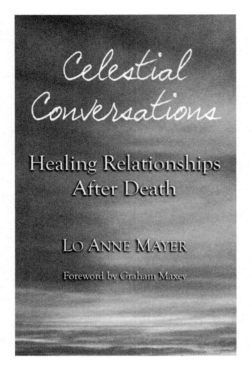

Printed in Great Britain
by Amazon